COLLECTED POEMS

POETRY

The Fivefold Screen
Visiting the Caves
The Dorking Thigh
A Shot in the Park
Taste and Remember
Celebrations

NOVELS

Turbott Wolfe
Sado
The Case is Altered
The Invaders
Museum Pieces

SHORT STORIES

I Speak of Africa
Paper Houses
The Child of Queen Victoria
Four Countries (Selected Stories)
Curious Relations (with Anthony
    Butts)

BIOGRAPHIES

Cecil Rhodes
The Diamond of Jannina

AUTOBIOGRAPHIES

Double Lives
At Home

FOR CHILDREN

The Butterfly Ball and the Grass-
    hopper's Feast (with Alan
    Aldridge)

LIBRETTI (WITH
    BENJAMIN BRITTEN)

Gloriana
Curlew River
The Burning Fiery Furnace
The Prodigal Son

EDITED

Kilvert's Diary 1870–1879 (3 vols)
Japanese Lady in Europe, by
    Haruko Ichikawa
A Message in Code: The Diary of
    Richard Rumbold, 1932–1961

COLLECTED POEMS

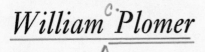

William C. Plomer

Jonathan Cape Thirty Bedford Square London

First published 1973
Collected Poems © 1960 by William Plomer
Taste and Remember © 1966 by William Plomer
Celebrations © 1972 by William Plomer
This collection © 1973 by William Plomer

Jonathan Cape Ltd, 30 Bedford Square, London WCI

ISBN 0 224 00809 9

Printed and bound in Great Britain
by Richard Clay (The Chaucer Press) Ltd, Bungay, Suffolk

PREFACE

When my *Collected Poems* came out in 1960 they were arranged in categories rather than chronologically. They now reappear with the addition of the poems in two later books, *Taste and Remember* (1966) and *Celebrations* (1972). It has seemed best to reprint these as they stood, not to classify them under the various headings in the *Collected Poems*, although they too include, for example, portraits, elegies, ballad-like pieces, epigrams, and African or other recurrent motifs. The two later books, left intact, can be seen therefore as later phases of one man's verse-making.

As it is now more than half a century since I began to write it might be thought fitting for me to enlarge here a little upon my beliefs and aims, although these must be implicit in the poems. I have read a great many prose utterances about poetry by valuable poets of various nationalities and periods up to the present, and where they have helped to clarify my own thoughts I have occasionally copied passages into notebooks for re-reading. However much these poets have theorized, and however brilliant or true or subtle their understanding (and they all seem somehow to share the same instinctive understanding of what poetry is) those for whom poetry is an art and not a mere foible are chiefly and naturally remembered by their poems.

When I was a boy, Ezra Pound thought (though I didn't know it at the time) that the poetry of this century would 'move against poppycock' and be harder and saner; as for his own work, he hoped that it would be 'austere, direct, free from emotional slither'. I hope I have myself moved in that direction. For an Englishman of my origin and upbringing, and of my generation, almost coeval with the century, there was a lot of poppycock to move against, not only in poetry; there were enormous encumbrances of accepted ideas about everything, and from these a man of my temperament and destiny had to struggle, largely alone, to free himself. To what extent the struggle has been reflected in my poetry I leave it to others to judge. What is clear is that for me the struggle has never involved anything so impossible and absurd as a reckless total rejection or denial of the past.

'Are *all* your poems about people?' a young questioner asked me after a poetry reading. A great many of them are. I have always been fascinated by certain patterns of the behaviour of particular persons in particular times and places, especially in the nineteenth century, to which belonged those who gave me birth and brought me up, and in the twentieth, to which I belong. This fascination, which in my earlier years caused me to produce novels, short stories, and to make one or two incursions into biography, has later found its point of focus in poetry.

Boys of my sort of upbringing were taught that poetry must obey strict rules of metre, rhyme, and propriety. We had to find out for ourselves that, as Nicanor Parra has said, *En poesiá se permite todo* – on certain conditions. I am not one of those who have felt able to abandon themselves to what Randall Jarrell called 'iron spontaneity', which he believed, and I believe, to be alienating to poetry. I would not think for a moment of despising or condemning the revolution which has made poetry popular in new ways and has helped the young to recognize and proclaim their own desires and fears, but the fashion for the public declamation of poetry does seem to tune in with the general tendency for the arts to become a part of show business, and for the distorted personality of the artist to be valued more than the work of art itself.

When Anna Akhmatova was in this country she said she thought that the tremendous success of some of the younger poets in Russia as what she called concert-hall performers had little to do with literature. Some of them, she said, tended to become captives of their own audiences, waiting for applause and beginning to write for applause. Long before that Jean Cocteau had remarked that the poet's real vocation was invisible, that he must walk along the dark side, and keep to the edge of the great main roads: in former times publicity had not tried to force into view what ought only to be seen at a distance in time, like starlight.

Does it follow from this that a poet who lives and works privately, making his work as exact and untrivial as he can, will in our time ruin himself by reading in public and enjoying the responses of audiences to what he reads? If he is constantly alert to the danger of making some sort of actor or exhibition of himself, and of trying to live up to the false personality into which publicity can easily transform him, I see, by the example of some

6

of my contemporaries, that ruin can be narrowly avoided, and I hope I have avoided it myself. So long as I feel myself still capable of 'awe, imagination, and tenderness' (the phrase is Charlotte Brontë's) I shall hope to feel that I have not betrayed my responsibilities to the written word and to those who may read or hear me.

W.P.

CONTENTS

CELEBRATIONS

AFRICAN POEMS

Three Poems of Johannesburg

SINGING IN THE BATH

With thick white arms
And a sip-syrup voice
The typist in her bath
Is able to rejoice,
Unlike the coloured man
Being led away to gaol,
His heart with insult bruised,
His skin with terror pale.

NOTE: An early utterance (1920) revised. Heavy-boned, fortyish, handsome in her way, the typist had a coarse skin, large pores clogged with powder, and hair dyed a brassy orange tint. She had a South African accent of such extreme refinement that it hardly seemed possible. Voice and accent were conspicuous among her secondary sexual characteristics, and were used to fascinate a business man with whom she would perhaps have welcomed – and for all I know attained – a formal union. She used to sing 'Tea for Two' in her bath.

17

CONQUISTADORS

Along the Rand in 'eighty-five
The veins of gold were torn,
Red houses rose among the rocks –
A plundering city was born.

Some who under the diamond stars
Had sailed the gilt-edged veld,
Wearing across their prow-like breasts
The order of the cartridge-belt,

Above their dream-entangled beards
Had steely, rock-drill eyes,
Cash-box conquistadors,
Anarchs of enterprise!

Some stole or cheated, some
Made off with their feverish gains,
And many failed, and a foolish few
Blew out their bankrupt brains.

Pioneers, O pioneers,
Grey pillars sunk in real estate,
How funny when the years have turned
Swashbuckler prim and scamp sedate!

Too late in memory's recesses
To find the nuggets of your prime,
Or recover the payable ore of youth
From the worked-out reef of time.

A FALL OF ROCK

Where not so long ago the breezes stirred
The summer grasses, now
A fat contralto gargles for applause
And bows in sequins when the curtain falls.

A sudden tremor shakes the theatre
And 'Oh!' cry two or three, while red and blue
Sparks fly from diamond earrings; several men
Are glad of an excuse to squeeze white hands
And murmur reassurance in small ears.
They say perhaps it was a fall of rock
In the deep mines below.

Perhaps it was a fall of rock. The city stands
On shafts and tunnels and a stinking void,
The bright enamel of a hollow tooth.
Where springbok bounded screams the tram,
And lawyer, politician, magnate sit
Where kite and vulture flew and fed.
Where the snake sunned itself, white children play;
Where wildebeest drank, a church is built.

Perhaps it was a fall of rock. Two kaffirs trapped
Up to the waist in dirty water. All the care
That went to keep them fit – !
Concrete bathrooms and carbolic soap,
A balanced diet and free hospitals
Made them efficient, but they die alone.
Half stunned, then drowned,
They might have lived in the sun
With miner's phthisis, silicosis,
A gradual petrifaction of the lungs.

If anybody imagines that ever
All this will come to an end,
That the jackal will howl on the ruined terraces

Of this city where science is applied for profit
And where the roar of machinery by night and day
Is louder than the beating of all the hearts of the inhabitants,
Far louder than the quiet voice of common sense;
If anybody should think that a mile below ground
The moling and maggoting will cease, or console himself
For his own failure to share the life of the city
With romantic hopes for its ruin,
He is wasting his time.

Do not let him suppose
That a bad future avenges the wrongs of now,
And let him remember
There is a fine gold to be won
By not always knowing best.

A BASUTO COMING-OF-AGE

The winter sun, a distant roar of light,
Immensely sets, and far below this place
Cold on the plains the vast blue tides of night
Press on, and darken as they race.
Out of retreat, with dancing and with dirges,
Men bring a boy in whom a man emerges.

The new man sees anew the twisted aloes,
His father's house, his cattle in the shallows,
And up the hill a crowd of girls advancing
To carry him to drinking and to dancing –
His heart leaps up as he descends the steep,
For, where the boy slept, now the man shall sleep.

NOTE: Why 'dirges'? Not funeral chants, but old tribal songs which, to a white
ear in a mountain solitude, may bring a sensation of intolerable melancholy.

THE DEATH OF A ZULU

The weather is mild
At the house of one of the dead.
There is fruit in the hands of his child,
There are flowers on her head.

Smoke rises up from the floor,
And the hands of a ghost
(No shadow darkens the door)
Caress the door-post.

Inside sits his wife, stunned and forsaken,
Too wild to weep;
Food lies uncooked at her feet, and is taken
By venturing fowls:
Outside, the dogs were asleep,
But they waken,
And one of them howls:
And Echo replies.

At last, with a sudden fear shaken,
The little child cries.

NAMAQUALAND AFTER RAIN

Again the veld revives,
Imbued with lyric rains,
And sap re-sweetening dry stalks
Perfumes the quickening plains;

Small roots explode in strings of stars,
Each bulb gives up its dream,
Honey drips from orchid throats,
Jewels each raceme;

The desert sighs at dawn –
As in another hemisphere
The temple lotus breaks her buds
On the attentive air –

A frou-frou of new flowers,
Puff of unruffling petals,
While rods of sunlight strike pure streams
From rocks beveined with metals;

Far in the gaunt karroo
That winter dearth denudes,
Ironstone caves give back the burr
Of lambs in multitudes;

Grass waves again where drought
Bleached every upland kraal,
A peach tree shoots along the wind
Pink volleys through a broken wall,

And willows growing round the dam
May now be seen
With all their traceries of twigs
Just hesitating to be green,

Soon to be hung with colonies
All swaying with the leaves
Of pendent wicker love-nests
The pretty loxia weaves.

THE SCORPION

Limpopo and Tugela churned
In flood for brown and angry miles
Melons, maize, domestic thatch,
The trunks of trees and crocodiles;

The swollen estuaries were thick
With flotsam, in the sun one saw
The corpse of a young negress bruised
By rocks, and rolling on the shore,

Pushed by the waves of morning, rolled
Impersonally among shells,
With lolling breasts and bleeding eyes,
And round her neck were beads and bells.

That was the Africa we knew,
Where, wandering alone,
We saw, heraldic in the heat,
A scorpion on a stone.

THE EXPLORER

Romantic subject of the Great White Queen,
See him advancing, whiskered and serene,
With helmet, spectacles, and flask of brandy
(That useful stimulant, he always keeps it handy),
Unmoved by cannibals, indifferent to disease;
His black frock-coat rocks sadly in the tropic breeze.

He never shows emotion, least of all surprise.
Here nothing meets his pale, protruding eyes
But big game, small game, fur and fin and feather,
And now he dreams of oatmeal, Scotland and the Flag,
The nimble corncrake in his native heather,
The handy corkscrew in his leather bag.

THE PIONEERS

The street, the store, the station, especially the bar,
Show what the fathers of this tin-town Main Street are:
Moustaches waxed, these mammoths lean on counters,
Old rotting whales ashore and thick with flies,
Their blubber proof to bullets and to kicks,
Fill up their guts and blow out spouts of lies,
Tales of rebellions, cannons and encounters,
Before their brains dried up in Nineteen-Six.

24

THE BIG-GAME HUNTER

A big-game hunter opens fire once more,
Raconteur, roué, sportsman, millionaire and bore –
But only shoots his mouth off, knowing how
He's safer on a sofa than on far safari now.

THE BOER WAR

The whip-crack of a Union Jack
In a stiff breeze (the ship will roll),
Deft abracadabra drums
Enchant the patriotic soul –

A grandsire in St James's Street
Sat at the window of his club,
His second son, shot through the throat,
Slid backwards down a slope of scrub,

Gargled his last breaths, one by one by one,
In too much blood, too young to spill,
Died difficultly, drop by drop by drop –
'By your son's courage, sir, we took the hill.'

They took the hill (Whose hill? What for?)
But what a climb they left to do!
Out of that bungled, unwise war
An alp of unforgiveness grew.

25

THE RUINED FARM

A peaceful, archangelic sun
Sank low, grew larger to the sight,
And drew across each huge ravine
The huger curtains of the night;

Silence within the roofless house
Undid her hair and shook it free,
The footpad jackal passed her there,
And bats flew round the cactus tree;

Each quiet afternoon was bitter,
Was overcharged with warning,
And Silence waited where the snake lay coiled
And mocked at each mild, bright morning.

ULA MASONDO'S DREAM

In a gorge titanic
Of the berg volcanic
A dark cave was hidden
Long untrodden.

There leopard and snake
And tawny partridge
Prey and are preyed on,
Unstartled by cartridge,
Where never a gun
Echoing shocks
The listening rocks;
Where in winter
When the granite crags
Receive the sun,
Far down, far down,
In the sombre forest
Under thin ice
The waters splinter
In flakes of fire,
And in shallow pools
The shadow of a hawk
Tense above the tree-tops
Quivers like a fish
Among the shadows
Of basking fishes.
When those parapets shimmer
In the morning in summer
The antelope turns
From the heat of the height
To a stream in the ferns,
Bounding unhurried
From sun to shadow:
There the lory wings scarlet
His way at noon; twilight
Rustles with bats;

And at dawn the cliff
Frowns with eagles;
There the wild cats
Crouch and tremble,
And hear the screams
Of the furtive jackal.

The cavern is hidden
In leaves and branches:
For centuries now
No avalanches
Have scarred the steep.
The cavern can keep
Its secret in stillness,
In darkness, enfolded
In the wild fig trees,
Whose sinews are moulded
To the curves of the stone,
And whose roots are thrust
In a crevice of dust,
Clinging tightly within
To the veins of the quartz,
And fed on the secret
And tasting-of-stone
Dews of the desert,
While their leaves unshaken
Are stirred by lizards,
A refuge for spiders,
An arbour for birds,
That gouge the soft fruit
And swoop into space
With thin stabs of music
In a hollow of silence.

On windless nights
When the cave is deserted
By the last baboon
The shafted radiance

Of the risen moon
Illumines like a lamp
The vaulted roof,
Where the moss is damp
And beaded with black
Dews bled from the rock,
Illumines like the ray
White and deific
Of an enormous Eye
This tongueless place
With light terrific.
In the flare and the hush
Appear the painted
Walls. Look, the art of
Hunters who were hunted
Like beasts by men!

Now the air is tainted
With a sudden whiff
Of distant carrion,
And the silence shrills
With the urgent quills
Of vultures soaring
From their look-out cliff,
Ready to feast
On dead man or dead beast.

But the silence returns
And moonlight floats,
And the Eye returns
To men before us
In time before ours,
Whose love and hunting
Are calcined in the blaze
Of light like chalk.

Far off, far off,
Where are the savage
Cities of the future?

When these colours fade
And lichens hang in their places,
When these forms lose their graces,
When these lines are not lines,
Blighted and bitten
By the gradual acid
Of rhythmic ages,
O up then and out
And over the placid
And azure sky of midday
Will take their way
These naked hunters
With their slow-stepping women
Stained with rose-ochre
Proudly proceeding
In prancing procession
With the eland and the gnu,
While each coloured
Courser canters
With the zebra and emu,
Giraffe and zebu,
Hunters and hunted
Flying forlorn,
Faint, faded, and few,
Far off, far off,
In the equal blue.

What are you doing,
Ula Masondo?
Do you follow the Bushmen?
Are you lost in the hollow
Root of the city?

NOTE: A dream must be allowed its own logic, but this dream requires a little
elucidation, especially as it is taken from its context in *Ula Masondo*, a prose
fiction. Ula Masondo, a youth from Lembuland, goes to Johannesburg to work
in the gold mines. One day he is trapped, deep underground, by a fall of rock.
Before he is rescued he dreams of a Bushmens' cave in the mountains of Lembu-
land. He and other boys discovered it. He had heard of the extinct Bushmen,
who decorated it with paintings. The idea of their extinction becomes now
mingled or confused with the idea of his own possible extinction.

30

THE VICTORIA FALLS

These are the Victoria Falls, whose noisy gushing
Attracts a noisy and a gushing crowd
Who rush from every country in the world to gape
At this cascade that is the usual shape.

Over the brink a lot of water slops
By force of gravity, and many a tourist stops
And stares to see a natural law fulfilled
And quantities of water that never stop being spilled.

These are the Victoria Falls, the brightest trinket
In the globe-trotter's box of well-worn curios:
If they want water, good God, let them drink it!
If they want falls, we'll knock them down – here goes!

Why do you come, I wonder, all this weary way?
Is it because you like to smile and say
'When we were at the Falls the other day – '?
Is it because you like to see the spray?

Is it because you like to feel how far
It is from Boston to these falls of the Zambesi,
Which must be falling still? Or do you feel uneasy
Until you know how like their photograph they are?

A female tourist raves, 'We're keen as keen
On Africa! It's dusty – but, my dear, the *sun*!
I had a list of all the things we've seen,
I can't remember half the things we've done!

'The Kaffirs? Black as black, they live in such quaint kraals –
They're dusty, too! The great thing is to see the Falls,
The rainbows, and the Rain Forest, where we all wore mackin-
    toshes,
Admired the ferns, and were so glad we'd all brought our
    goloshes!'

(The water spirits leered at her, the lurking *tokoloshes*.)
'My dear, the spray! the noise! the view! the beautiful hotel!
Electric light in every room, and an electric bell!
So clean and comfortable, and they looked after us so well!'

She will not go away ... Ach, I long to be alone
With a guide-book to the gentle Falls of Silence,
The Temple of Reticence on the Tranquil Islands,
Where no sound enters, whence no sound goes out,
And waterfalls
   Fall
      Quietly,
         As tea falls
            From
               A spout.

NOTE: *Tokoloshes*. Mischievous or malignant bogies or goblins in Bantu
mythology.

THE DEVIL-DANCERS

In shantung suits we whites are cool,
Glasses and helmets censoring the glare;
Fever has made our anxious faces pale,
We stoop a little from the load we bear;

Grouped in the shadow of the compound wall
We get our cameras ready, sitting pensive;
Keeping our distance and our dignity
We talk and smile, though slightly apprehensive.

The heat strikes upward from the ground,
The ground the natives harden with their feet,
The flag is drooping on its bamboo pole,
The middle distance wavers in the heat.

Naked or gaudy, all agog the crowd
Buzzes and glistens in the sun; the sight
Dazzles the retina; we remark the smell,
The drums beginning, and the vibrant light.

Now the edge of the jungle rustles. In a hush
The crowd parts. Nothing happens. Then
The dancers stalk adroitly out on stilts,
Weirdly advancing, twice as high as men.

Sure as fate, strange as the mantis, cruel
As vengeance in a dream, four bodies hung
In cloaks of rasping grasses, turning
Their tiny heads, the masks besmeared with dung;

Each mops and mows, uttering no sound,
Each stately, awkward, giant marionette,
Each printed shadow frightful on the ground
Moving in small distorted silhouette;

The fretful pipes and thinly-crying strings,
The mounting expectation of the drums
Excite the nerves, and stretch the muscles taut
Against the climax – but it never comes;

It never comes because the dance must end
And soon the older dancers will be dead;
We leave by air tomorrow. How
Can ever these messages by us be read?

These bodies hung with viscera and horns
Move with an incomparable lightness,
And through the masks that run with bullocks' blood
Quick eyes aim out, dots of fanatic brightness.

Within the mask the face, and moulded
(As mask to face) within the face the ghost,
As in its chrysalis-case the foetus folded
Of leaf-light butterfly. What matters most

When it comes out and we admire its wings
Is to remember where its life began:
Let us take care – that flake of flame may be
A butterfly whose bite can kill a man.

After Thirty Years

A TRANSVAAL MORNING

A sudden waking when a saffron glare
Suffused the room, and sharper than a quince
Two bird-notes penetrated there
Piercing the cloistral deep verandah twice.

The stranger started up to face
The sulphur sky of Africa, an infinite
False peace, the trees in that dry place
Like painted bones, their stillness like a threat.

Shoulders of quartz protruded from the hill
Like sculpture half unearthed; red dust,
Impalpable as cinnamon softly sifted, filled
With heaped-up silence rift and rut.

Again those two keen bird-notes! And the pert
Utterer, a moss-green thrush, was there
In the verandah-cave, alert,
About to flit into the breathless air.

The strangeness plucked the stranger like a string.
'They say this constant sun outstares the mind,
Here in this region of the fang, the sting,
And dulls the eye to what is most defined:

'A wild bird's eye on the *qui vive*
Perhaps makes vagueness clear and staleness new;
If undeceived one might not then deceive;
Let me', he thought, 'attain the bird's eye view.'

IN THE SNAKE PARK

A white-hot midday in the Snake Park.
Lethargy lay here and there in coils,
And here and there a neat obsidian head
Lay dreaming on a plaited pillow of its own
Loops like a pretzel or a true-love-knot.

A giant Python seemed a heap of tyres;
Two Nielsen's Vipers looked for a way out,
Sick of their cage and one another's curves;
And the long Ringsnake brought from Lembuland
Poured slowly through an opening like smoke.

Leaning intently forward a young girl
Discerned in stagnant water on a rock
A dark brown shoestring or discarded whiplash,
Then read the label to find out the name,
Then stared again: it moved. She screamed.

Old Piet Vander leant with us that day
On the low wall around the rocky space
Where amid broken quartz that cast no shade
Snakes twitched or slithered, or appeared to sleep,
Or lay invisible in the singing glare.

The sun throbbed like a fever as he spoke:
'Look carefully at this shrub with glossy leaves.'
Leaves bright as brass. 'That leaf on top
Just there, do you see that it has eyes?
That's a Green Mamba, and it's watching *you*.

'A man I once knew did survive the bite,
Saved by a doctor running with a knife,
Serum and all. He was never the same again.
Vomiting blackness, agonizing, passing blood,
Part paralysed, near gone, he felt

'(He told me later) he would burst apart;
But the worst agony was in his mind –
Unbearable nightmare, worse than total grief
Or final loss of hope, impossibly magnified
To a blind passion of panic and extreme distress.'

'Why should that little head have power
To inject all horror for no reason at all?'
'Ask me another – and beware of snakes.'
The sun was like a burning-glass. Face down
The girl who screamed had fallen in a faint.

TUGELA RIVER

1

The river's just beyond that hill:
Drive up that track!

Look, isn't that someone standing there?

Yes, someone old and thin,
Some old witch perching there,
Standing on one wasted leg
With scaly skin, and taking snuff.
Unwanted, old and thin,
And waiting for the end,
She'll smell of ashes, and have no good news.
The skimpy rag she wears,
A cotton blanket once,
Protects her with its colour, not with warmth;
It has the dusty, ashen look
Of winter, scarcity, and drought.
Bones in a blanket, with a spark of life
Nothing by now can fan to flame,
Old hag, why don't you move?

36

It's not a woman, after all –
Only a thorn bush all disguised with dust!
Ah well, in this clear light
Things often are not what they seem,
Persons are often things,
Fear takes on form,
Delusions seem to have
The density of facts:
Kick one, and see!

It's just a thorn bush in a web of dust,
A statue of powder in this windless glare.
But, all the same, I shouldn't speak to it:
It might reply.
Silence itself might crack
Into an eerie cackle, dry and thin
As all this sapless winter grass,
Deriding us out of the lost past and out
Of what will be the past, when we are lost.

We've passed her now – or rather, *it*.
There, down the hill, the river in its bed,
Tugela River, seems as quiet
As this dead pythoness in her dusty fur.

White light, dry air, an even warmth
Make for well-being, tone and calm
The nerves, the blood.
No cloud, no breeze;
Clear as the focus of a burning-glass
But wholly bearable, the sun
Is fixed upon us like an eye.
We seem enclosed inside a vast
And flawless plastic dome
As for some new experiment.
We shall not know if we have passed the test,
We don't know what it is.

I feel we cannot fail.
The river in this still
Gold morning will renew our strength;
Reduced by drought
It does not show its own,
Only its constancy.
Look, turn off here, and park above that rock.

2

Tugela River! Thirty years ago
These same eyes saw you at this very place
Just at this time
Of winter, scarcity, and drought:
Not that you know or care;
But nothing is unrelated, wasted, lost.
There is a link
Between this river and that boy,
A boy obliged to learn
Subjects not mastered all at once –
Patience, and energy, and rage.

The hard earth cracked, the river shrank,
The boy came here because the river knew
Answers to questions.

Juiceless as straw, the glistening grass
Brittle and faintly gold
Waited for fire.

Then came the time of burning of the grass:
At night the veld-fires drew
Their mile-long arcs of jerking flame
Under the smoky stars.
Fences of dancing fire
Crackled like pistol shots,
Pricking new frontiers out
Into the passive dark.

It seemed the field by night
Of one of the those miscalled
Decisive battles of the world,
With cannon smoke and musket fire,
A master plan, and screams of pain
As some to-be-renowned outflanking move
Destroyed a long-established power
With crowns and crosses on its ancient pinnacles.
Morning revealed the hills mapped out
(Yesterday's straw-pale hills)
With empires painted black!

Burnt veld-grass had a sad and bitter smell
Like letters kept, then burnt,
Like battles fought, and lost –
No, battles fought and won!

3

Eastward and constant as a creed
Tugela swam,
The winter river, much reduced,
Past shaped alluvial clean white sand,
Past stalks of maize upright but dead
In hillside patches poorly tilled
By dwellers under domes of reeds
Who by their poverty seemed to expiate
Their furious past.

Cool, cool Tugela slid
Haunted with unwritten myth,
Swam like a noble savage, dark
And muscular in shade, or clear
In the sun an emerald angel swam.

As sleek as oil Tugela poured,
And paused in pools,
And narrowing lapsed
Below the rigid erythrina trees

39

That held their carved and coral flowers
Like artifacts against the arid sky.

And farther down, down there,
Funnelled through channelled rocks
To rapids and cascades, kept up
A white roar of applause
In the still brightness of an empty day.

4

Rivers of Europe with a cross of gold
In liquefaction at the inverted point
Of wavering dome or undulating spire,
Printed with dimnesses of trees
And redolent of mist and moss,
Reflect what looks like peace.

There, seated idols in a row,
The anglers on the bank
Catch something less than peace.
They never catch the gold reflected cross:
It ripples, breaks, re-forms, and melts.
No anglers here, fishing for peace.
Look at that pool, a glass
For nothing but the shadow of a rock.

It was a glass once for a Zulu youth –
I saw him standing on that rock
His fighting-sticks put by –
Who on a concertina improvised
A slow recurrent tune, subdued
By want of hope, yet with the stamping feet
The drums of hope
Beyond the horizon, and its just-heard song.

I know his family. They tell me he was found
Dying of inanition in the sun
On a road verge, while new cars

Hissed past like rockets
Loaded with white men hurrying like mad,
While he lay on the dark red earth
With all his youth subdued.

5

It is to be misled
To think his death was final, as to think
The river that you see, the dried-up grass,
Will stay like that;

Or that a race of men locked up and ruled
In a delusion built by psychopaths,
Locked up and staring at the floor
Between their patient feet,
Are there for good.

If, after thirty years, in winter calm
Tugela gliding as before might seem
Merely an unnavigable stream
Idling for ever in the gold
Dry atmosphere, remember this:
Patience erodes.

Here where we stand
Through the rich grass of summer there will pour
A press and pride of senseless force,
Roar like a mob, a tidal wave
Shaking its mane, and overturning rocks
Fulfil the promise of catastrophe.

When patience breaks, the sinews act,
Rage generates energy without end:
Tugela River, in the time of drums
And shouting of the war-dance flood
Will break a trance, as revolutions do,
Will promise order, and a future time
Of honey, beer, and milk.

THE WILD DOVES AT LOUIS TRICHARDT

Morning is busy with long files
Of ants and men, all bearing loads.
The sun's gong beats, and sweat runs down.
A mason-hornet shapes his hanging house.
In a wide flood of flowers
Two crested cranes are bowing to their food.
From the north today there is ominous news.

Midday, the mad cicada-time.
Sizzling from every open valve
Of the overheated earth
The stridulators din it in –
Intensive and continuing praise
Of the white-hot zenith, shrilling on
Toward a note too high to bear.

Oven of afternoon, silence of heat.
In shadow, or in shaded rooms,
This face is hidden in folded arms,
That face is now a sightless mask,
Tree-shadow just includes those legs.
The people have all lain down, and sleep
In attitudes of the sick, the shot, the dead.

And now in the grove the wild doves begin,
Whose neat silk heads are never still,
Bubbling their coolest colloquies.
The formulae they liquidly pronounce
In secret tents of leaves imply
(Clearer than man-made music could)
Men being absent, Africa is good.

NOTE: Louis Trichardt is a town in the Northern Transvaal.

POEMS WRITTEN IN JAPAN

THE DEATH OF A SNAKE

['Death and generation are both mysteries of nature, and somewhat
resemble each other.'   *Marcus Aurelius*]

Bruised by a heel he strove to die,
In frantic spirals drilled the air,
Turned his pale belly upward to the sky
In coitus with death: and here and there
Scored in the dust quick ideographs of pain –
These, that the wind removed, in memory remain.

WHITE AZALEAS

Mats of woven grass
  In the lighted room
    Where he lay in bed;

All at once he heard
  The audible-by-night
    Bamboo waterfall;

Shadows of the trees
  Were moving on the ground
    Underneath the moon.

Midori came back
  With a hiss of silk,
    And knelt upon the floor,

In her golden hand
  A branch of white azaleas
    Crystal-dropped with dew.

45

Two Hotels

NOTE: It was still possible in the nineteen-twenties, especially in remote country places, to feel the presence of Japan's past, and to feel it intensely. The Aburaya was an ancient inn in the central mountains of Japan. Its appearance had altered little since the days when the Daimyos, or feudal noblemen, paused there, with processions of retainers, on their way to Yedo (Tokyo). Its ancient timbers, carved and painted with phoenixes, peonies and other decorative motifs, retained some splendour, and the manners, deportment and beliefs of the family who owned the place could have altered little from those of their ancestors. From the windows could be seen, not far away, the then dormant volcano, Mount Asama, and, over grey tiles encrusted with gold lichen, the flowery fields of summer, from which was wafted the smell of thyme. For the sake of the rhythm, it is important to remember that the stress on each syllable of the Japanese place-names is equal.

The completely different picture of what was then a modern hotel in the port of Yokohama, rebuilt after the great earthquake of 1923, speaks, I believe, for itself.

THE ABURAYA

1

A hare-lipped hag beneath an ancient gable,
Where the phoenix and the peony have yielded to the spider and
    the bat,
Puts by her broom of twigs, stands up as straight as she is able,
Sniffs, is swallowed by a cave-like doorway, and is followed by
    the cat.

She never notices the path before the door wants weeding,
No visitor arrives from September until June,
Then only tired students laboriously reading
While the mist uncovers Asama to the once volcanic moon.

Lacquer in the daimyo's room is overlaid with dimness;
On the door beneath a worm-holed architrave
A faded gilded swallow skims a curly stylized wave –
Only with words as patinous could a hushed voice limn this
Silence of decay in an odour of the grave.

46

2

One family has lived here since pre-processional days,
Buddhists of the Zen sect, splitting meditative hairs,
Pleased to be obsequious when the building was too small,
And now it is too big content to stare at a blank wall,
Ready for the retinues of emperors or nobody at all,
Drifting with the fatal and erratic eddies of affairs.

Placidly a window-screen is opened by the landlord's daughter,
A buxom rustic poetess of seventeen –
Very sentimental, smelling clean
As a white chrysanthemum in a glass of water.

The subjects of her verses are in the usual taste,
Conventional without dullness, and without coldness chaste:
The taste of the sound of silence in the snow,
The vanishing of the twilight shadows of a pine-tree on a lonely
    beach,
The scented oblivion of the voices of those who were lovers
    long ago,
And the sense of the irreparable in an opening flower of peach.

3

Though once it buried Rokuri-ga-hara under planetary lava-
    banks,
Nobody considers Asama a menace; nobody forgets
That this has been the road to Yedo; nobody remembers
Men no longer carry swords. The daughter of the house
Smiles gently, sad with inexperience and inarticulate regrets,
And rising from the household circle crouching round the embers
Sometimes slips away, forgetting her grandfather and all,
To stand on a balcony towards the south
And watch the maple leaves or first few snowflakes fall –
And at such a time she sings with a small and virginal mouth:

'Near the ruined castle of Komoro
   Travellers by twos and threes
      Hasten through the spring haze
         With the barley showing green
            Through the melting snow;

'A bamboo flute; the wrinkled waves
   Of the river Chikuma
      Far below – a dreary day,
         But on my pillow of grass
            At the inn above the cliff
               I am a little content.'

HOTEL MAGNIFICENT
(Yokohama, 1927)

['If you long to mingle with Cosmopolitans in Yokohama amidst gorgeous
Oriental pageantry, fill out and mail the information blank below.'
                    Contemporary American advertisement]

Where stout hunters unbamboozled by the stoutest of bamboos
Suck icy liquors up through straws or strut in patent-leather shoes,
While tourists of both sexes bandy-legged or bald as bandicoots
Hobnob with Hollywood's who's-who or dally with cheroots,
Stranger, look round, or stand and listen to the band.

Japan, they say that Kipling said, is 'not a sahib's land',
But *si sahib requiris, circumspice* in the well-planned grand
Brand-new Hotel Magnificent whose highly-polished floors
Reflect both millionaires and brassy pseudo-Jacobean cuspidors.

Descend with despatch to the Daimyo Dining Room
('Takes the tired tourist back to stirring Feudal Days'),
Fashioned all in Burmese teak and like an Aztec magnate's tomb
Well it has deserved a drunken baseball-champion's praise.

'Old-world craft,' with New World craftiness
The new prospectus says, 'continually ply
Beneath these very windows' – but the naked eye
Sees nothing more than motor-boats beneath a smoky sky.

The pergola pillars on the roof are hollow,
Made of cement and steel and topped with whirring cowls
To ventilate the kitchens ninety feet below
And a corridor to the ballroom where a loud-voiced gossip prowls:

'She says they say they may go from here to San Diego
Or Spain by aeroplane or out into the blue;
On the fat wife of a dago seed-pearls look like small sago
But she certainly asserts he is a personage in Peru.'

Here East meets West to the strains of *The Mikado*
Born kicking from the strings of a Filipino band
Whose members have an air of languor and bravado,
And one a Russian emerald lucent on his hand,
A trophy of the ups and downs, the switchback way we go,
Pressed upon a supple finger by an exile starving in the snow.

The band strikes up again and from bedroom and bridge-table
In this modern Tower of Babel people glide towards the door;
The band bursts out anew, and a wistful nasal whining
With hypnotic syncopation fills the ballroom's glossy floor
With two-backed beasts side-stepping, robots intertwining,
Trying to work a throwback, to be irresponsible once more.

AT LAKE CHUZENJI

'The best July resort in the whole Far East'
So he was told, the stout Bombay Greek
Watching the water, clear and still as aspic.

The yacht race this morning looks like yesterday,
White isosceles triangles on parallels sliding
Passing and repassing, he wonders to what end.

V within V behind a motor boat
The splay waves spread and waver, a German lady swims,
Down comes the rain and voices interpenetrate.

'We ought to go and see that beastly waterfall.'
'Who is this young man that follows her round?'
'Three hearts.' 'And you?' 'I pass.' 'What's yours?'

A sudden yearning for an evening with geisha
Cruises along his hardening arteries,
But sadly he turns his broad back on the lake,

Resigned to missing intimacy with Japanese joys,
To no longer being young, and to not being free
From his wife, his daughter, his hotel, or propriety.

AUTUMN NEAR TOKYO

A pear, a peach, a promenade,
September sheds the first red leaf
Between tall millet rows
A stooping woman reaps.

Persimmons fatten overhead
And thin blue smoke aspires
To fade into the paler sky.
Still hardly cool the evening comes.

A dusky freshness and the sweet
And musky cheapness of a cigarette
Hang on the fading air. The old
Are thinking of the past.

Emphatic through the mist
Twangs the strong samisen;
Those taut strings struck
In a light top room

Are struck for us, the young!
Arrows into the night
That bowstring song lets fly,
Our longings to be strong!

THE GINGKO TREE

Chrome-yellow in the blue,
   Tremolando tree,
Flute-like aquarelle,
   Pure fragility.
   When the sun
Faded in a misty wind
   Branches spun,
   Scattered clear
Propaganda, quickly thinned
   Turning twigs,
   Leaves untwirled –
Parasol or pamphleteer.

NOTE: Although gingko trees can be seen in England, the leaves in autumn do
not turn so pure and bright a yellow as in Japan.
   A tall gingko tree in the grounds of a temple is dressed in its bright yellow
foliage, dazzling in clarity and delicacy. In the evening a wind gets up and the
leaves begin to fall, suggesting leaflets thrown from a window or an aircraft.
The wind causes them to fall in spiral eddies, which produce an illusion that the
trunk of the tree is revolving, and the branches seem like the framework of a
twirling parasol.

TWO LIKE ONE

Dry grasses whistle on the cliff.
The driven sand tattoos
Patterns of pain on hands and face.
Huge waves attack. Tatters of froth
Sail through the air. The long-haired rocks
Drip icicled with running crystal tunes.

Crouched on a log like one an ancient pair,
Their driftwood bundles by, themselves wrapped up
In age-use-moss-mould-mottled rags.
Dull detonations signal bursts of spray.
Against this battle habit is their shield –
They sit inside it like a shell they've grown.

JAPONAISERIE

O la douce vie insensée!
The early sun accentuates
Green lettuces on rime-white soil
With shadows glowing blue.

A sparrow leaves a springboard twig
And powdered sugar falls: look up
Where arsenal chimneys trace
Sky-writing slow on frozen air.

The sacred Fuji, pale as pearl,
Is ruled across with telegraph wires –
Moi mandarin, toi mandarine,
Nous irons, souriant un peu.

NOTE: The title is ironical. The silly lines in French are taken from a senti-
mental 'Oriental' piece by a writer whose name I have forgotten. They came into
my head in a wintry landscape, with its evidence of heavy industry. I find the
opinion expressed, thirty years later, that I was a pioneer in writing of the
Japanese 'without exoticism and without condescension'. (Earl Miner, *The Japanese
Tradition in British and American Literature*)

THE PAULOWNIA AVENUE

Night in a car of jet
    With iron-grey horses flew,
Leaving like a stage all set
    The avenue.
Under the antlers all disguised with leaves
    Was carried swaying
Minamoto Yoritomo the fratriphobe
    Pale with spleen.

Day in a car of coral
    Rose to view,
And without delaying
He lifted the gold curtain of the palankeen
    To give the trees a look,
Whereupon the wind-ruffled corymbs of flower-bells
    Powdery blue
With papery muttering shook.

NOTE: Minamoto Yoritomo became Shogun towards the end of the twelfth century.

For an educated Japanese the paulownia has heraldic and historic as well as aesthetic and personal associations. Even to a stranger it here evokes the past.

There is nothing Japanese about the car of jet and the car of coral. They are here to help to suggest the haste of an ambitious and powerful statesman up to no good.

'Antlers' refers only to the shape of the branches. There is no allusion to cuckoldry or deer.

A MOMENT OF PEACE

Lulled on the Yellow Sea
   Long lacquered afternoons
Idly loll the refugees
   From the maniac typhoons.

Muffled rolling satin deep,
   Early night, a star breeze
Stirs the peonies on the slope
   And the sleeping Annamese.

Underneath the folded sail
   Its photograph in monochrome
Wavers, and the evening lull
   Saddens, like a dream of home.

PHILHELLENISMS

ARCHAIC APOLLO

Dredged in a net the slender god
Lies on deck and dries in the sun,
His head set proudly on his neck
Like a runner's whose race is won.

On his breast the Aegean lay
While the whole of history was made;
That long caress could not warm the flesh
Nor the antique smile abrade.

He is as he was, inert, alert,
The one hand open, the other lightly shut,
His nostrils clean as holes in a flute,
The nipples and navel delicately cut.

The formal eyes are calm and sly,
Of knowledge and joy a perfect token –
The world being caught in the net of the sky
No hush can drown a word once spoken.

THE YOUNG BRIDEGROOM

[*From a Greek original*]

On the west side in the white room
That reflects a new morning
In the white bed the young bridegroom
Is asleep still, she sees him
Sleeping like a lamb.

Daytime, and the young bride
Wishes to wake him,
But not with a sprinkle
Of water – it might chill him;
And not with a tipple
Of wine – it might bemuse him.

So she takes a sprig of basil
And strikes him with the sweet herb
Lightly on the lips:
'The sun's up, my golden one,
All the nightingales are silent!'

DISTICHS

[From Greek originals]

1

Curse you, plane-tree, for your leafiness –
The girls fetching water can no longer be seen.

2

Want me as I want you, and as I love, love me –
Or the time may come that you'll love me when I want you no
more.

A LEVANTINE

A mouth like old silk soft with use,
The weak chin of a dying race,
Eyes that remember far too much –
    Disease, depravity, disgrace
    Have worked upon that face.

And yet the mask of slow decay
Outbraves the pride of bouncing fools.
As an old craftsman sighs to hear
    His name neglected in the schools,
    And sees the rust upon his tools,

Through shades of truth and memory
He tunnels, secret as a mole,
And smiles with loose and withered lips,
    Knowing the workings of his soul
    Had something in them sound and whole.

61

With Socrates as ancestor,
And gold Byzantium in his veins,
What if this weakling does not work?
    He never takes the slightest pains
    To exercise his drowsy brains,

But drinks his coffee, smokes and yawns
While new-rich empires rise and fall:
His blood is bluer than their heaven,
    Poor, but no poorer than them all,
    He has no principles at all.

THE LAND OF LOVE

Kalirrhoë Kalogerópoulos, widow, keeps a café
At the supposed site of the Serangeion baths,
A small pink house under a fragrant fig-tree
Built into the cliff-face and reached by goat-track paths.

'The Land of Love' is the name of the café;
It is well named, for the terrace night by night is
Frequented by at least two or three pairs of lovers
And the bathing-booths below are also Aphrodite's.

In the evening one enjoys thin resined wine, then
(A beggar with a guitar going by in the gloom)
The black currant-grapes that are eaten by bunches,
Red mullet with pepper, and a powdered *loukoum*.

Loukas, Vasili, and Nestor, municipal clerks,
Used to come here by tram when melons were ripest;
Loukas was drowned, diving among the moon-flakes,
And Vasili shot Nestor on account of a typist.

THE PHILHELLENE
(Athens, 1930)

Round about Athens
In the strangest fashions
Strolls the harridan
    Of whom I speak;
Of American origin
She has long been foraging
In Attic byways
    And has gone all Greek

In a pseudo-classical
Boston, Mass-ical,
Quite fantastical
    Kind of way,
Looking art-and-crafty
And slightly draughty
In a homespun chlamys
    Of a greeny-grey:

Athenian loungers
And touring strangers,
I fear, all find her
    A figure of fun,
With her skin weatherbeaten
And her bony feet in
Sandals, and her coiffure
    A filleted bun.

She crossed the ocean
Long ago with a notion
Of expressing emotion
    In rhythmic poses
And of living sparsely
On bread and parsley,
But the simple life was
    No bed of roses;

She had plenty of dollars,
But felt that scholars
Alone could master
    Classical Greek,
The enclitic particle
Quite defeated her
And declining the article
    Left her weak;

Then one Papayannópoulos
Took her up the Acropolis
And began to monopolize
    Most of her time,
He said he was a poet
And in order to show it
This guileful Adonis
    Addressed her in rhyme.

His favourite tense was
The Present Erotic
And he taught her the demotic
    Speech of to-day,
With his bold airs and graces
He put her through her paces,
They did things and went places –
    She was quite carried away!

So, alas, was her fortune!
To hear him importune
Her for more drachmas
    Melted her heart;
Each time re-enchanted
She gave him what he wanted,
So he feathered his nest and
    Left her in the cart.

Deserted, this Aspasia,
This threadbare Ophelia,
Grew dowdier and crazier,
    A solitary freak,

And in fancy dress she lingers
With a locket in her fingers
Containing a curl from
    That xenophil Greek.

CORFU

The fig divides where mortar bound
The bastion and the parapet,
Fennel and sage and grasses wave,
No gunsmoke drifts across the bay,
This is a view without a war.

Across the old fortezza fall
The crystal rulings of the rain,
The moon above Albania burns
Fitful as a brigand's fire,
And no boat passes out to sea.

Cloud-light dazzles with cliffs of peace
The tranced Homeric afternoons,
The sea tumbles pale and dark,
A gull wheels, and a clock counts four
Not heard by ears that earth has filled.

Empty at night the shuttered square,
Lightning shakes the tall pink town,
Turkish, Venetian, English hearts
Have stopped beneath the struggling wind,
The wrestling trees and wetted walls.

In lamplight the magnolia leaves
Blink wet with rain and metal-bright,
At the old fort the lighthouse beams
Its constant warning north and south
Smoothly, to keep Ulysses from the rocks.

THREE PINKS

Crisp hair with a faint smell like honey
Hived by fierce bees under a fallen column in a pinewood,
A liquor of wild oleanders in a limestone gully –
Although it is summer there is snow on Parnassus –
Crisp hair awoke me, brushing my cheek.

Open your eyes, undo those modest fringes
Under the eyebrow-arches, wide, Byzantine, black,
White-wine coloured eyes in a rose-tan skin,
Antique young eyes! Smile, my primitive,
Fill the hushed air with amusement and secrecy,
And you need not, with such fine teeth, forbear to yawn –
And with such sweet breath.

                         Still half awake
We shall get up together from the bed
And with arms interlaced cross to the window
(The early morning is cool and heavenly),
Then standing mutely look out over a quiet
Aspect of Athens, rococo houses and stucco
With a cypress or two in the middle distance
Like marks of exclamation at such tranquillity.

See, in the exsiccate light of Attica
The pepper-tree garden where last night by full moon
An old woman disturbed our intimacy
To sell us three pinks with long stems.

See now, the Acropolis is still unsunned.
Forestall dawn with yet one more kiss,
Last of the night or first of the day –
Whichever way one may chance to choose to regard it.

ANOTHER COUNTRY

'Let us go to another country,
Not yours or mine,
And start again.'

To another country? Which?
One without fires, where fever
Lurks under leaves, and water
Is sold to those who thirst?
And carry drugs or papers
In our shoes to save us starving?

'Hope would be our passport;
The rest is understood.'

Deserters of the vein
And true continuousness,
How should we face on landing
The waiting car, in snow or sand,
The alien capital?
Necessity forbids.

(Not that reproachful look!
So might violets
Hurt an old heart.)

This is that other country
We two populate,
Land of a brief and brilliant
Aurora, noon and night,
The stratosphere of love
From which we must descend,

And leaving this rare country
Must each to his own
Return alone.

GOOD-BYE TO THE ISLAND

Good-bye to the island
And the view across the straits:
Work that gained us pleasure
Will now be done by others.

Good-bye to the pleasure
And the island girls
Who taught us as they fancied
And found us willing learners.

Good-bye to the fancies
Of two wandering boys,
The picnics on the mountain
Where the grass was gilt and brittle.

Good-bye to the ruins,
The tramway to the port,
The dusty moonlit suburbs,
The private rooms we rented.

A life of wine and marble
And voices in the mist
Will trouble us no longer,
The gulls are all returning.

The past was like a sculptor
Determining our will,
We grapple with the future
And shape our new intentions,

So now to the last harbour
And our easygoing ways,
To white grapes in a basket
And the island nights, good-bye.

TWO PORTRAITS

CAPTAIN MARU:* A NATIONALIST

1

Meet Captain Maru, used to being obeyed,
The servant of a monarch called a god.

Urbanity, and such a feline smile,
And evidence of power in control,
Did they not seem beguiling when there danced
A trellis of reflected light upon the ceiling?
Calm, perhaps the calm of rarest mastery –
Could the young resist this navigating friend?

Maru, with culture at his elbow like a wine,
An autocrat as host, smiling but reserved;
Maru to a lady offering a gift
Tied with white and scarlet, the perfect samurai
With a pattern of blossoms on his sword;
Maru being boyish with a boy; astute,
Learning to treat women in the Western way;
Maru at the self-possessed narrowing his eyes –
Could the young resist? The voyage had begun.

Twin screws of ambition drive the hull
And Maru heads the table and the ship,
Abbot of its drilled, monastic life.
With much to teach and learn, he shows
That Maru is commander of himself.

At judo is unbeaten, in the hold
Armoured and visored, a ferocious fencer,
He wins on points: the trimmers watch,
The second engineer retires. Each afternoon,
The course set northward and the ship
Breasting the tropic swell, Maru's alone

* On both syllables the stress is equal.

Fresh from the bath, to chant the classics,
A deep-chested dirge, a stylized howl,
And later silence, to exercise his soul.

Does he relax? He does. The shogun bends.
The man of iron is still a man of moods,
Takes relaxation seriously too.
The lips unclench: a slightly gilded smile.
Maru in his cups does a sword-dance on the deck,
Bare-legged, with feet as vigorous as hands,
With a whole ocean for a private room,
Stamps and shouts according to old rules,
His face all flushed and big veins in his neck,
And muscles, eyes, and anger all belong
To a follower of Saigo, a Kumamoto tough.

He fought at Kilindini with a corpse for weapon.
A flat-faced lad from snowy Echigo fell dead,
Peasant, ship's carpenter, then body to be buried –
But where? Not white: but our nations were allied.
Two days of Maru, then a surplice and a bell,
A slow bell and a surly gown, the crew in white
Under the saw-toothed palms, a shallow grave,
Pink sunset, distant gramophone, white flowers,
Heads turned, and honour satisfied, and Maru wore
The sure smile of a victory of the will.
'And thou shalt have
None other race but mine.'

2

Maru as a traveller always cool and clean,
Debonair in his many ports of call
With white silk suit, topee, and gold-topped cane,
Chose his words carefully, got what he required,
Exacted deference by being firm and calm.
The envoy of an emperor keeps his head,
Saves face, shakes hands, bows, does not yield ...

Never so firm as when he met the great rebuff,
Which may have been imagined.
Nothing more was said. He put a photograph away.
With fumes of resentment clouded like a glass,
Was wrapped in silence that said, *But we can wait.*
The pride and hatred duty breeds
Condensed inside his strong heart's caves,
Pride grew another shell, gall gained a drop,
Determination hardened a formidable man.

Maru in Malaya and later in Macao,
Man of affairs and condescending guide,
Despised the Chinese and their choice of pleasures,
Sneered at their music, 'a degenerate mode',
But praised their cooking. Maru off Sumatra
(The sea a plain of polished lead
Pitted with rain, the mountain tops
Dense with green jungle, soaked in thundercloud)
Became urbane, explained a chart, recalled
Hazards and faithfulness in war.

3

Focused in a porthole gliding rocks and pines:
Is this the promised land with the cold green wind
The stiff trees comb till they hum?
With the polished Russian shells on pedestals of stone
And the plangent notes from cat-gut guitars
Twanging like bowstrings in the ancient wars?

Maru claps his hands, will conjure up a proof
Here, best of all, is pleasure understood.
'Here only is the brothel clean, the courtesan a wit,
Here only are the sheets of silk, the talk refined;
The right wine rightly warmed, the best food served,
The garden planned with due symbology
And the room centred on a calligraphic scroll
From the brush of an adept in the art of self-control.'

73

The drunkard wallows: Maru sits upright.
The girls are giggling: Maru only smiles,
And crossing to the windows sees the moon
And quotes a verse about an octopus
Caught, in the thirteenth century, in a trap.

And now the city, where the birth-rate chokes
The trams and streets, but Maru navigates,
Purposeful day and night, using the press,
The radio, banquets, interviews, the great
To serve his various ends.
The Foreign Minister rises from his desk,
Cordial but cautious, one eye on the clock.

So much for that, and Maru has a week
Before he sails again, and so he turns,
Takes train to a quiet place on the coast,
For Maru is of course a family man
And skipper of an ever-growing crew
Of little Marus full of national pride.
There only at evening, by the Inland Sea,
Is Maru tender, like a girl with dolls
Handling his young, whose little gowns
Are wreathed already with the blossoming sword.
As virile husband to a docile wife, he thinks
He serves the glory of the State,
Ignorant that he is helping to provoke
Death chemical from fleets with wings.

4

Maru at home, in an old gown and clogs
Scrambling along the rocky shore;
Or Maru standing all night on the bridge
The third night running and the fog no less;
Or Maru as a good companion, sharing
The lives of younger men for a day or two,
With charm, perhaps the charm of one who feels

Just for a time that he is really free,
Until the little stings are felt
Of disapproval, disappointment, destiny –
These Marus mix with others,
Maru neglected where his hopes were huge,
Or Maru bitten by a stalking-horse,
Or Maru's knuckles white with rage repressed,
Maru resigned and covering his scars,
Back on the bridge, and in the afternoons
Singing some elegy of ancient wars,
A cultivator of his faculties
And calm – but not the calm of rarest mastery.
And now he has appeared to someone in a dream
Or rather a nightmare, menacing, a giant,
With no back to his head, uttering a taunt –
It is the challenge of his race, the short man scorned,
Not satisfied with power, but mad for more.

NOTE: A portrait of a Japanese nationalist between the two World Wars.

Section 1, line 13. Everything in Japan symbolizes something else. The cherry blossom signifies 'the spirit of a true Japanese', that is, in Maru's interpretation, a militant patriot.

Line 42. *Saigo Takamori*, a hero of remarkable character, led the reactionary Satsuma Rebellion in 1877. He came from Kumamoto, a town in Kyushu, the southern island. Its inhabitants had long prided themselves on their virile, patriotic and warlike traditions and habits.

Line 43. *Kilindini*. A harbour in East Africa.

Section 3, line 4. *Russian shells*. Relics of the Russo-Japanese War converted into memorials, and to be seen in the grounds of some Shinto shrines.

Last line. *Death chemical*. A forecast of the bombing of Japan during the Second World War.

75

JOHN DREW: A VAGABOND

1

A low laugh of delight, and a young cheek stained
Like a sea-pink by the wet winds of the county Mayo
Distinguish John Drew in the city,
To self-pity a stranger, and a stranger too
In the pale-faced, smut-bound Cockney crowd.
From Westport in Mayo that fertile voice
And the long-boned arms, rakers of ribbony kelp
That drapes the westward rocks when the breakers fall back,
And the black hair the rain wind blew over the eyes
Their candour now rimmed with a fog-borne ophthalmia.

What is London to him but a place on his way
Where he finds work or lacks it, lies down
On a hard bed or soft or no bed at all?
Where on a wet day he dined off a pig's head in a cook-shop,
Entered a library to learn the intrigues of our governors,
And a wash-house to get rid of the grime,
Sluicing his lean flanks with steaming carbolized water,
As a stranger encountered a stranger
Who knew him, recognized his low laugh of delight?

That he 'wandered abroad' was a charge brought against him
'Without visible means of subsistence':
Slept in a train at a siding. Bound over.
He wanders abroad, no enemy of society,
Entered by him at points where a need is mutual
To make a new road or load up the new-mown hay,
To do odder jobs than those, in short
To give and get for a day or a month what he can;
Subsists by the work of his hands, and the chance to continue.
Another time he was drunk, too drunk for decorum,
And his visible means of subsistence was joy.

76

Many a man has found peace in a conflict,
Loved hating, submitted with pride:
Has not each his own paradox? John Drew
Finds constancy, balance, in change and caprice.

2

Atlantic all night long across the park
The storm tormented trunk and branch,
Drops pattering in the dark like shot.
The wind at full pressure, suddenly less loud,
Was an enemy shoulder trying to force the door
Of the keeper's cottage, where Drew lay sleeping
His head on his arm, his face with a flush
Like the ripening stain on the sunward side of a fruit,
He who in August in those ferny rides
Caught rabbits and a glinting, coppery pheasant.

In the morning he left, grateful and singing,
Glad of kindness and the calm silence
And the lights of the town he would reach that evening
Gay-pointed already in the highways of his forward blood.
The rubber-frilled fungus he struck from a stump
With a stick, treading soft in the leaf-muffled glade,
The winter-stripped wood; and stood and looked up
At the rainwashed, red-fruited holly.
Let that be his badge, the evergreen holly,
Ripe in the dimness of rainy December,
Rich in the bareness of bark colonnades,
The branch of goodwill brilliant in gloom.

He refreshes himself in the rays of surprise,
This nomad, this casual citizen
Who will never buy a house by instalments
Or lift up a child of his own with his powerful hands;
His hair will go grey but will never be laid
Alongside the wedded grey of an old woman's head;
As a fumbling old man John Drew will be found

In a workhouse twilight, end of a winding route
Which would make, mapped out, an intricate hieroglyph,
The lacy and looped arabesque of a personal quest.
No daughter will close his eyes, and no fond hand
Ease the old pains of one who once lived for new pleasures –
But remember: John Drew is free.

How is he free, since no one is free?
Of parents now dead, his offspring unborn
Even in the secret seeding-places of the heart
(For John is weak in the stir to nest and hive)
Does he live for himself alone? Does any man?

He finds in our calm and moderate island
(Land of the bank, the pulpit, and the flag,
So neatly balanced between facts and dreams,
The outlaw Irish and the reasoning French)
Scope for his gait, who stoops and smiles.
When order is prose, then error is a song,
Then some find freedom in the right to smile
And a sneer is an intellectual thing.
To be a critic when the rest create
Or a creator when the rest conform,
To be a rebel, in ambush on the road
To ready-made Utopias, with a gun,
To die at will, when others live by rule,
Is sometimes freedom: so far Drew is free.

3

Keep out the winter, John Drew, winter the leveller,
Stripper of all that each separate branch puts out;
Keep fresh that blue, that curious, smiling eye
That notices, wonders, enjoys, and wants to know:
Keep the power of appraisal; and may your hand
With padded, work-worn fingers gentle and strong
Keep its love for what is fitting and shapely.
Taker of casual ways, tramp whom some have respected,

Unconcerned to reform other people,
Uttering a low laugh at makers of by-laws,
Fresh as a sea-pink where the asphalt ends,
Remain yourself: you have proved
That to be oneself is a kind of greatness.
Remain yourself, like the evergreen holly seen
At the end of a woodland ride at the end of December,
Glossy flourisher among bone-like trunks,
Berry-bearing yielder of the festival branch
And rainwashed wreaths of delight.

A TIME OF PRISONS AND RUINS

EPITAPH FOR A CONTEMPORARY

A cold new wind came bustling up the street,
Agitating the hair on the lifeless head
Of a young man face down in the gutter;
He lay where he fell, shot by a sniper.

He was not shot for opposing the revolution;
He had seen that it had to happen.
Did nothing against it, held his tongue,
Then, hearing the first bombs explode, sighed.

He was rash enough to go out for a breath of fresh air;
He loved freshness and was tired of the nerves and cigarettes
Of partisans and non-partisans crowded in rooms
And the priggish claptrap of doctrinaire know-alls.

Shot through the stomach, he took time to die;
His face, contorted with the effort of dying,
Grew calm, and in death perhaps had a certain nobility,
But nobody saw his agony or his looks.

In any case, he was lying face downwards;
His point of view had always been earthbound,
A good dinner pleased him more than a new star discovered,
And vivid exceptions more than rules imposed.

When he was born, there were quite enough stars in the sky;
When he died, there was too much blood in the streets,
This immoderate world of too much or too little
He did not expect to be changed overnight.

His parents had money at one time, and lost it,
But they did not complain or pity themselves;
This they owed to ancient habits of mind
Very far from the dogmas of the revolution.

His trouble was, they brought him up a gentleman,
And when he grew up, he found it didn't pay,
But it was too late to alter his character,
To learn to assert himself or mispronounce vowels.

It was no longer the fashion to be gentle;
Because he had manners he was thought proud,
Manners were out, only new things were reverenced;
For respecting old virtues he was thought half mad.

After his father died, his mother was restless;
Wearing carved antique beads she walked up and down,
But their clacking annoyed her, and she took them off
As if she had no right now to such adornments.

Her son begged her to put on the necklace again,
The sound pleased him, as in his childhood,
A soft telling of the rosary of inexhaustible affection,
The kind, comforting, elegant, maternal monomania.

Somehow there was a fatal charm in that sound;
It may be much easier to go back where you came from
Than to go all alone and do what you are not used to,
To break ties, to fall foul, to pioneer and grow hard.

Perhaps this was why the young man achieved little.
Ah, well, his time was not wasted. If he was robbed
His money was certainly taken by people who needed it,
And that cannot always be said of those who are robbed.

It was wonderful to be so clear and calm,
Wonderful how he saw through things and people
And yet often loved them. 'So brilliant,' was said of him,
'But there seems to be very little to show for it.'

He at one time dreamed of having some power
Not to enrich himself or domineer over the gullible,
But to show himself magnanimous and earn gratitude;
Such vanity, however, necessity made him outgrow.

He was too soft in fibre, wanting in coldness,
Afflicted with disbelief and a failing of hope,
Hated his time, took drugs, spoke in a quiet voice,
And lived in the margin, watching onrushing life.

His wilful affections had a life of their own;
Those that wanted to love him he could not love,
And those he loved were always the very ones
Who wondered why he loved them so much.

His own light guided him, but an undue sense
Of his own unimportance in the scheme of things
Made him reckless at times – a saunterer on battlefields
Cannot expect his peregrinations to last.

Nature seems to waste much to make little;
Enormous and complex processes went to make him,
And yet he himself was one of the discarded
And ended up in the gutter, face down in the mud.

It may be that he died with resignation;
Over the death-pangs life comes leaping,
And perhaps at the end he heard, or imagined,
The half cruel, half playful laughter of children.

THE RUINS

Snapped off and earthquake-scattered
Segments of Corinthian columns lie
Fluted like celery-stalks in stone
Buff-biscuit on the desert grey.

Some stand, supporting yet
Fragments of pediments soon to fall.
Acanthus capitals can be kicked
Out of the sand like fossils. Surely

No moral need be drawn from this?
Bright poisonous gourds have coiled
Over the vast cylinders, but these
Small wild musk-melons ought to quench our thirst.

NOTE: In other words (though other words will not do), when traditional beliefs
have collapsed, and the broken remains of tradition are half covered with
oblivion and half hidden by noxious new growths, it does not follow that all
new growths are noxious: some of them may be life-giving and delightful.

THE SILENT SUNDAY

From the bandstand in the garden on the hill
Where workless seamen moped on benches
And shrieking children worked the swings
The wide curve of the estuary can be seen.

Half-way down the hill a murder case
Once drew idle crowds to stare
Over the mottled laurels in the garden of an inn,
And a newspaper stood up on end
And moved unsteadily, urged by the wind,
Like a child that learns to walk.

That busy world of cars and bungalows,
Who would have thought that it would stop so soon?
Fissures appeared in football fields
And houses in the night collapsed.
The Thames flowed backward to its source,
The last trickle seen to disappear
Swiftly, like an adder to its hole,
And here and there along the river-bed
The stranded fish gaped among empty tins;
Face downward lay the huddled suicides
Like litter that a riot leaves.

They say some women lived for weeks
Hidden in bushes on the common, then drew lots
And ate each other. Now
A sunny mist hangs over everything.
An almond tree suggests that this is spring
But on the right an oak retains its leaves.

Where are the sea-birds? Why no gulls?
All drowned when the oil-tanks burst?
Water chuckles from a broken pipe.

THE PRISONER

Every morning the prisoner hears
Calls to action and words of warning:
They fall not on deaf but indifferent ears.

Free speech, fresh air are denied him now,
Are not for one who is growing thin
Between four walls of Roman thickness.
From his cell he sees the meetings begin,
The vehement lock on the orator's brow
And the listeners warped by want and sickness.

His old wound throbs as old wounds will,
The summer morning makes his head feel light,
Painful the sunlight on the whitewashed sill,
Trembling he awaits the ever-fruitful night,
For then dreams many-formed appear
Teeming with truths that public lips ignore,
And naked figures struggle from the sea
Shipwrecked, to be clothed on shore,
And words no orator utters are said
Such as the wind through mouths of ivy forms
Or snails with silver write upon the dead
Bark of an ilex after April storms.

While flights of bombers streak his patch of sky,
While speakers rant and save the world with books,
While at the front the first battalions die,
Over the edge of thought itself he looks,
Tiptoe along a knife-edge he slowly travels,
Hears the storm roaring, the serpent hiss,
And the frail rope he hangs by, twisting, unravels,
As he steps so lightly over the abyss.

IN THE NIGHT

When the pillowed head instead of sleeping ponders
The night is given shape by noises half expected
And freed from untrue light imagination wanders
To find the shape of life in violence recollected.

The tower clock in striking tells not of time so clearly,
When on the air we breathe impinge those bronze vibrations,
As of the lives we lead and ways we cherish dearly
Shaken by sudden fears and wounding revelations;

As of those shocks of pleasure, a phrase, an act forbidden,
That an infant hoarded up, his secret and his treasure,
Guides to later conduct, clues to wisdom hidden,
Truer than clocks or calendars as rules by which to measure.

Startling here a folded thought, an impulse uninvited,
Streets away an engine screams, starting for the west,
At the tremor nerves respond, as a bulb when lighted
Suddenly reveals a room whose existence was unguessed.

By a parting, by a journey, by adventure yet unknown
Though already understood by a shadow cast ahead
We discern in part the pattern of the lives we lead alone
Faithful to designs bequeathed us by the dead.

Eternity's blue flesh seen through a cloud in tatters,
Voices in a villa garden, and an open door,
For a moment seem familiar, then the vision scatters,
Memory seems to seize on something somehow known before.

And the future *is* the past in the head upon the pillow,
The eye rests on a landscape where the heart will throb,
A house by a canal, a white wall, and a willow,
Remembering what has not happened ... Do you hear a sob?

We bleed from others' wounds; for our own the styptic
Is not time, no healer for the heart that grieves,
But resistance to surprise and acceptance of the cryptic:
And now the night wind sighs abruptly in the leaves.

IN A BOMBED HOUSE: AN ELEGY IN MEMORY OF ANTHONY BUTTS

[The following stanzas commemorate the last male descendant of one branch of an English family rich in tradition and notable for its associations with remarkable men, among them Henry VIII, Holbein and Bacon. One member of the family is a character in Shakespeare, another helped to found a college at Cambridge, another was the friend and patron of Blake. Two distinguished themselves in battle, one at Poitiers and one in the Crimea: the latter was among the first to be recommended for the Victoria Cross, but declined the honour on the ground that all his men, to whom it had not been offered, deserved it equally. In this family a peculiar mixture of pride and modesty made for indifference to worldly honours, and this trait, together with originality and intellectual curiosity, recurred to the end. Its last representative had uncommon talents but was temperamentally unable to develop them with the persistence which makes for fame.]

The raid is over and the feverish night
(War's a debauch for which our heirs must pay),
A chair is smashed, the floor is strewn with glass,
        Each fragment bright with day:

Not this nor any other day will bring
That dear familiar (quizzical, urbane)
Who found life wonderful, acquitting man
        As guilty but insane.

He was a true eccentric, understood
Nothing of money but the joys it brings,
Loved the bright fuss of wordly luxury
        And bold imaginings:

Selecting words, or colours with a brush,
Sometimes he caught a strangely clear effect,
Like the chance images of passing life
        That lonely lakes reflect:

90

And his the talker's gift, myth after myth
Brilliant from banal scenes he drew
(Flags of all nations from a juggler's mouth)
    Unending into view.

But he was an exile in his own country
As many noble Englishmen have been:
The glowing eye grew coldly critical
    Of the unhappy mean,

Distasteful of a duller England where
Suburban civilization ruled at last
A people tamed to obey the *comme il faut*,
    Untrue to their great past;

He saw the stranded gentry run to seed,
The workless poor who never got a start,
And stuck-up ignorance preening in the glass
    Of academic art;

He heard the huge machines of *force majeure*
Tune up for murder, while the tourists lay
Tanning their torsos on the summer coasts,
    Sunning their brains away:

Over the world he went – in search of what?
Beauty and truth, perhaps, that shop-soiled pair
Of vague ideals, asked more of life, perhaps,
    Than life can spare;

Java, Jamaica, Riga, Istanbul
Gave him his moments, drove him home again –
He also drank the sun, and then came back
    To London in the rain.

A dilettante with a watchful eye,
Who served the world because he could admire,
Negroes he loved, and next to Negroes, paint
    Which warmed him like a fire;

91

Europe he loved, a Europe of his own,
And saw it fall into a fierce decline,
And in his vitals too the rot set in –
    He was part of the design:

But courage was his, the kind that seems to prove
The soul is something separate after all,
And danger made him calmer, he who could
    Foresee but not forestall,

Courage that throws the body like a glove
At grinding Fate that crushes in its stride
Man, concrete, harebell – Fate, the tank
    That never turns aside.

And so when sickness sapped his life away,
Weak, wasted, waxen, risen from the dead,
He clothed his bones, and turning from his last,
    His doctor-haunted bed,

He worked for war, who hated war, and died.
The blind or seeing hand that shoots or steers
Is nerved with hope: so was that active head
    Through all these murderous years.

As in a waste of seas the cruising shark
Follows a raft, and never turns aside,
Death followed him. But love was following too,
    Was with him when he died.

BLIND SAMSON

Their mockery brought him double force,
They gave him (ruined by their gain)
Clear sight to see his destiny
And make their smallness plain.

The smallness of the seeming great
Taught him to make no compromise,
His anger smashed their mocking skulls
And stopped their grinning eyes.

POEMS OF THE AFFECTIONS

VISITING THE CAVES

Suddenly I discover in a wooded place
The trees are rooted in the hollow of your hand,
And when with finger-tips your veins I trace
See branching runnels in the firm sea-sand.

The lift, the gangway and the staircase lead to you,
And you, my bed and pillow, give me rest;
I visit the caves and am guided, and I know
Those galleries are glittering within your breast;
Whatever you receive I share
And I carry you like a passport everywhere.

Words are born between my fingers, you their source,
And the pen I hold is as delicate as a bone,
With you for compass I can steer a course
And with you for company can bear to be alone:
Bringing goodness out of complicated evil
The world (for me) you have raised to your level.

Your moorland strength sustains me in the street,
And the thought of you touches me as a plectrum strings –
Child, parent, mate, heart with a steady beat,
Yours is the warmth in which the future sings.

A LOST FACE

To seek a lost or missed face, and not trace it
Slides a screen of clear glass across street, grass and vista,
As for a huntsman killing for hunger not fun
Leaf and twig cruelly detailed and motionless
Seem in the know, conspiratorial,
Hiding fawn pelt of beast or grain-fattened bird
Dearer by disappearance, needed by the trigger finger,
The sharp-eyed stomach, and the children at home.

Seeking to trace the lost face, it seems untrue
That the tides of ourselves, in hats, shoes, and coats,
Ghosts lent substance, precarious hurriers
Whom death teases, neglects or surprises,
Should be able to conceal such features as those –
But look at the shallows: they shelter a kingfisher.

Hereabouts the treasure was buried
But the keen spade dredges up nothing but earth.
It is time to go home – unless suddenly the steel
Strikes metal, and vibrates like a tuning-fork.

THE BARREN PEARTREE

1

Late work that night before sleep
Under the homely thatch.
On the barren peartree near the door
Hung the carcase of a sheep,
And miles of desert mooncalm shone
While the busy meatsaw bit through bone.

The leaves and meat framed only this,
A mountain nicknamed Genesis,
Peak where no prophet yet has stood
Possessed, to speak with God,
His bearded throat raised up,
The moon reflected on his lip,
His straining eyeballs veined with red,
And his forehead carved like column-top
Helping uphold a dome.

No answer there but rock,
The lonely and reluctant echo,
The cry delaying, the unanswered cry,
Hollow, diffuse, and faint:
But the peartree was in bloom with light
Petalled with promise of future fruit.

2

It bears a handsome harvest: heavy like breasts
The fruits hang touching, ripe for hands.
Chasing two diamonds rolls a kinder moon
Through nightblue coolness and a pack
Of racing fleeces roselit from below,
Warmed by a town's endeavour,
Tints of a private, sure reward,
The harmony of give and take,
Trust, gratitude, restraint.

SEPTEMBER EVENING: 1938

As the golden grass burns out
In a cooling ash of dew
The lovers disembrace
And face the evening view.

The long plain down
Shaped like a thigh
Slopes towards the sea,
And away up in the sky

Too small to be heard
A purposeful silver spark
Bright in the sun's last rays
Glides eastward into the dark;

Plain as a stack of hay
In the valley at their feet
A primitive small church
Looks simple, strong, and neat:

Inside a wattled fold
An unsafe flock of sheep
Stand, stir, or lie
Fleece against fleece asleep;

Lights in a bungalow,
A constant hum of cars;
Mallow flowers in the grass;
One or two stars.

With the fading day
All has grown clear:
All is felt to be vital
And infinitely dear.

Looking round, the girl thinks
'How precious to me
My home and my work and each thing
I can touch and can see,

'George's navy-blue suit,
And my white linen dress,
And the way that his eyebrows grow –
This is my happiness!'

And he, clasping her hand,
More grave than before,
Says, 'Yes, I will fight
From no lust for war

'But for all that has gone to make
Us, and this day.'
Then arm in arm along the path
Silent they saunter away.

THE UMBRELLA

1

In the nocturnal city I needed no map.
The name of the street
And the number of the house,
I knew them like thirst:
So I found my way all right
    On that clear spring night.

I took with me all I had –
Body, head, heart.
It was too much to take –
How was I to know that?
All of me felt so light
    That soft spring night.

When I got to the house
No sign of a door!
But someone was there –
I saw a face look out
Through a window, straight into mine –
    But it made no sign.

I went all round the house
And back to where I began:
And now the windows had gone –
The façade was utterly blank
And all of the same grey brick,
    As if by a trick.

I had taken there all I had –
Most of all, hope.
Worse than a dream when the earth
Gives way, to be left
Standing with feet of stone
    On the granite street.

Taxi? Thank you, I said, I'll walk.
I felt on my skin the scab
Of drought. With paper and dust
I began an irregular drift
In continuing dusk –
    A dry, light, empty husk.

2

That was all long ago,
And I never went back.
A circuitous journey began –
Perhaps its hazards were part
Of an ultimate good
    Not then understood.

My dispersonate self once more
Drew on the gloves of flesh,
And it put on a pair
Of the spring-heeled shoes of hope:
To live, one has to defy
    What one cannot live by.

And healing came
On a thunderstruck day
With the drum of drops on a dome
Of shared black silk – thumps
Asserting in quickening rain
    Purpose was pulsing again.

NOTE: 'Constante *vagabondance* du désir – une des principales causes du
détériorement de la personnalité. Nécessité urgente de se ressaisir.'
                             (Gide, *Journal*, January 1912)

LONDON BALLADS AND POEMS

MISS ROBINSON'S FUNERAL

A cold afternoon, and death looks prouder
As mourning motors mourning motors follow,
One solemn as another. Lilies shiver,
Carnations also shiver, while the hollow
Seagulls search for offal in the river
And a woman burrows in her bag for powder.

The undertakers don't observe the scenery
And nothing moves them but the wheels they glide on,
The undertakers undertake to bury
(How black the motor cars they ride on),
They are not volatile or sad or merry,
Neither are waxworks going by machinery.

The coffin's full, and the time is after four;
The grave is empty, earth joins earth once more –
But the ghost of the late Miss Robinson is floating
Backside upwards in the air with a smile across her jaw:
She was tickled to death, and is carefully noting
Phenomena she never thought of noticing before.

A TICKET FOR THE READING ROOM

With a mile of secret triumph
   Seedy old untidy scholar,
Inkstains on his fingernails,
   Cobwebs on his Gladstone collar,

Down at heel and out at elbows
   Off he goes on gouty feet
(Where he goes his foxy smell goes),
   Off towards Great Russell Street.

Unaware of other people,
   Peace and war and politics,
Down the pavement see him totter
   Following his *idée fixe*.

Past the rowdy corner café
   Full of Cypriots and flies
Where the customers see daggers
   Looking from each other's eyes,

Past the sad but so-called Fun Fair
   Where a few immortal souls
Occupy their leisure hours
   Shooting little balls at holes,

Past the window full of booklets,
   Rubber goods and cures for piles,
Past the pub, the natty milk-bar
   Crowded with galactophiles,

Through the traffic, down the side-street
   Where an unfrocked parson thrives
('Palmist and Psychologist')
   Cutting short unwanted lives,

Through the shady residential
    Square in which a widow runs
A quiet gambling-hell, or 'bridge club',
    Fleecing other women's sons,

On he shuffles, quietly mumbling
    Figures, facts and formulae –
Bats are busy in the belfry,
    In the bonnet hums a bee.

At the Reading Room he settles
    Pince-nez on his bottle nose,
Reads and scribbles, reads and scribbles,
    Till the day draws to a close,

Then returns to oh, what squalor!
    Kippers, cake and dark brown tea,
Filthy sheets and filthier blankets,
    Sleep disturbed by mouse and flea.

What has the old man been doing?
    What's his game? Another book?
He is out to pour contempt on
    Esperanto, Vōlapük,

To fake a universal language
    Full of deft abbreviation
For the day when all mankind
    Join and form one happy nation.

In this the poor chap resembles
    Prosperous idealists
Who talk as if men reached for concord
    With their clenched or grasping fists.

109

MOVE ON

They made love under bridges, lacking beds,
And engines whistled them a bridal song,
A sudden bull's-eye showed them touching heads,
Policemen told them they were doing wrong;
And when they slept on seats in public gardens
Told them, 'Commit no nuisance in the park';
The beggars, begging the policemen's pardons,
Said that they thought as it was after dark –

At this the law grew angry and declared
Outlaws who outrage by-laws are the devil;
At this the lovers only stood and stared,
As well they might, for they had meant no evil;
'Move on,' the law said. To avoid a scene
They moved. And thus we keep our cities clean.

FRENCH LISETTE:
A BALLAD OF MAIDA VALE

Who strolls so late, for mugs a bait,
In the mists of Maida Vale,
Sauntering past a stucco gate
Fallen, but hardly frail?

You can safely bet that it's French Lisette,
The pearl of Portsdown Square,
On the game she has made her name
And rather more than her share.

In a coat of cony with her passport phony
She left her native haunts,
For an English surname exchanging *her* name
And then took up with a ponce.

110

Now a meaning look conceals the hook
Some innocent fish will swallow,
Chirping 'Hullo, Darling!' like a cheeky starling
She'll turn, and he will follow,

For her eyes are blue and her eyelids too
And her smile's by no means cryptic,
Her perm's as firm as if waved with glue,
She plies an orange lipstick,

And orange-red is her perky head
Under a hat like a tiny pie –
A pie on a tart, it might be said,
Is redundant, but oh, how spry!

From the distant tundra to snuggle under her
Chin a white fox was conveyed,
And with winks and leerings and Woolworth earrings
She's all set up for trade.

Now who comes here replete with beer?
A quinquagenarian clerk
Who in search of Life has left 'the wife'
And 'the kiddies' in Tufnell Park.

Dear sir, beware! for sex is a snare
And all is not true that allures.
Good sir, come off it! She means to profit
By this little weakness of yours:

Too late for alarm! Exotic charm
Has caught in his gills like a gaff,
He goes to his fate with a hypnotized gait,
The slave of her silvery laugh,

And follows her in to her suite of sin,
Her self-contained bower of bliss,
They enter her flat, she takes his hat,
And he hastens to take a kiss.

Ah, if only he knew that concealed from view
Behind a 'folk-weave' curtain
Is her fancy man, called Dublin Dan,
His manner would be less certain,

His bedroom eyes would express surprise,
His attitude less languor,
He would watch his money, not call her 'Honey',
And be seized with fear or anger.

Of the old technique one need scarcely speak,
But oh, in the quest for Romance
'Tis folly abounding in a strange surrounding
To be divorced from one's pants.

THE WIDOW'S PLOT:
or, SHE GOT WHAT WAS COMING TO HER

Troubled was a house in Ealing
Where a widow's only son
Found her fond maternal feeling
    Overdone.

She was fussy and possessive;
Lennie, in his teens,
Found the atmosphere oppressive;
    There were scenes.

Tiring one day of her strictures
Len went down the street,
Took a ticket at the pictures,
    Took his seat.

The picture was designed to thrill
But oh, the girl he sat beside!
If proximity could kill
    He'd have died.

Simple, sweet, sixteen and blonde,
Unattached, her name was Bess.
Well, boys, how would *you* respond?
    I can guess.

Len and Bessie found each other
All that either could desire,
But the fat, when he told Mother,
    Was in the fire.

The widow, who had always dreaded
This might happen, hatched a scheme
To smash, when they were duly wedded,
    Love's young dream.

One fine day she murmured, 'Sonny,
It's not for me to interfere,
You may think it rather funny
    But I hear

'Bess goes out with other men.'
'I don't believe it! It's a lie!
Tell me who with, where, and when?
    Tell me why?'

'Keep cool, Lennie. I suspected
That the girl was far from nice.
What a pity you rejected
    My advice.'

Suspicion from this fatal seed
Sprang up overnight
And strangled, like a poisonous weed,
    The lilies of delight.

Still unbelieving, Len believed
That Bess was being unchaste,
And a man that feels himself deceived
    May act in haste.

Now Bess was innocence incarnate
And never thought of other men;
She visited an aunt at Barnet
    Now and then,

But mostly stayed at home and dusted,
Crooning early, crooning late,
Unaware of being distrusted
    By her mate.

Then one day a wire was sent:
MEET ME PAELACEUM AT EIGHT
URGENT AUNTIE. Bessie went
    To keep the date.

Slightly anxious, Bessie came
To the unusual rendezvous.
Desperate, Lennie did the same,
    He waited too,

Seeing but unseen by Bessie,
And in a minute seeing red –
For a stranger, fat and dressy,
    A trilby on his head,

In his tie a tasteful pearl,
On his face a nasty leer,
Sidled up towards the girl
    And called her 'Dear.'

At this juncture Len stepped in,
Made a bee-line for the lout,
With a straight left to the chin
    Knocked him out.

114

He might have done the same for Bess
Thinking still that she had tricked him,
But she was gazing in distress
    At the victim.

'It's a *her*!' she cried (but grammar
Never was her strongest suit):
'She's passed out!' he heard her stammer,
    'Lennie, scoot!'

'It's *what*? A *her*? Good God, it's *Mum*!
Ah, now I see! A wicked plan
To make me think my Bess had come
    To meet a *man* –'

'Now what's all this?' a copper said,
Shoving the crowd aside. 'I heard a
Rumour somebody was dead.
    Is it murder?'

Len quite candidly replied,
'No, officer, it's something less.
It's justifiable matricide,
    Isn't it, Bess?'

MEWS FLAT MONA:
A MEMORY OF THE 'TWENTIES

She flourished in the 'Twenties, 'hectic' days of Peace,
'Twas good to be alive then, and to be a Baronet's Niece.
Oh, Mona! it's not so good now!

Mona in the first war was a Problem Child,
She roared and ranted, so they let her run wild;
Expelled from St Faith's, she was shot from a gun
At a circus she'd joined, for a bet, at Lausanne.
Oh, Mona! they're rid of you now!

She had her hair bobbed, when the fashion began,
To catch the eye of some soft-hearted man.
Oh, Mona! they're just as soft now!

A man was caught; she ran off in her teens
With the heir to a fortune from adding-machines,
But he failed to reckon up the wear and tear,
By the time she left him he had iron-grey hair.
Oh, Mona! you're subtracted now!

Mona took a flat in a Mayfair Mews;
To do that then was to be in the news.
Oh, Mona! it wouldn't be now!

The walls were of glass and the floor of pewter,
This was thought 'intriguing', but the bathroom was cuter;
On a sofa upholstered in panther skin
Mona did researches in original sin.
Oh, Mona! they're concluded now!

Mews Flat Mona, as a Bright Young Thing,
Led a pet crocodile about on a string;
In a green cloche hat and a knee-length skirt
She dragged the tired reptile till it was inert.
Oh, Mona! it's gone to earth now

116

Diamond bracelets blazed on her wrists
(They were not presented by misogynists)
And Mona got engaged to a scatterbrained peer;
His breach of promise cost him pretty dear.
       Oh, Mona! he couldn't pay now!

When she gave a dance she engaged three bands,
And she entered the Ritz once walking on her hands;
She drove round London in a crimson Rolls,
'The soul of every party' – as if parties had souls!
       Oh, Mona! the party's over now!

Mews Flat Mona, as a Period Vamp,
Spent a week end in a nudist camp;
Her barefaced behaviour upset the crowd
And she came back sunburnt under a cloud.
       Oh, Mona! you're in the shade now!

She babbled of Coué and also of Freud,
But her book of engagements was the one she enjoyed.
       Oh, Mona! you've no dates now!

She lived for a time with an Irish Jew
And thought it an 'amusing' thing to do;
He taught her to take morphia, heroin, and 'snow',
A giddy life, but she was used to vertigo.
       Oh, Mona! no pipe-dreams now!

Too bright were her eyes, the pace was too fast,
Both ends of the candle were burnt out at last.
       Oh, Mona! you're blacked out now!

She stepped from the top of an Oxford Street store;
She might well have waited a split second more
For she fell like a bomb on an elderly curate
And his life was over before he could insure it.
       Oh, Mona! you're exploded now!

When they came with a shovel to shift her remains
They found a big heart but no vestige of brains.
       Oh, Mona! that accounts for you now!

117

THE CALEDONIAN MARKET

A work-basket made of an old armadillo
  Lined with pink satin now rotten with age,
A novel entitled *The Ostracized Vicar*
  (A spider squashed flat on the title page),
A faded album of nineteen-oh-seven
  Snapshots (now like very weak tea)
Showing high-collared knuts and girls expectant
  In big muslin hats at Bexhill-on-Sea,
A gasolier made of hand-beaten copper
  In the once modern style known as *art nouveau*,
An assegai, and a china slipper,
  And *What a Young Scoutmaster Ought to Know* ...

Who stood their umbrellas in elephants' feet?
  Who hung their hats on the horns of a moose?
Who crossed the ocean with amulets made
  To be hung round the neck of an ailing papoose?
Who paid her calls with a sandalwood card-case?
  From whose eighteen-inch waist hung that thin chatelaine?
Who smoked that meerschaum? Who won that medal?
  That extraordinary vase was evolved by what brain?
Who worked in wool the convolvulus bell-pull?
  Who smiled with those false teeth? Who wore that wig?
Who had that hair-tidy hung by her mirror?
  Whose was the scent-bottle shaped like a pig?

Where are the lads in their tight Norfolk jackets
  Who roistered in pubs that stayed open all day?
Where are the girls in their much tighter corsets
  And where are the figures they loved to display?
Where the old maids in their bric-à-brac settings
  With parlourmaids bringing them dinners and teas?
Where are their counterparts, idle old roués,
  Sodden old bachelors living at ease?

Where the big families, big with possessions,
  Their standards of living, their errors of taste?
Here are the soup-tureens – where is the ambience,
  Arrogance, confidence, hope without haste?

Laugh if you like at this monstrous detritus
  Of middle-class life in the liberal past,
The platypus stuffed, and the frightful epergne.
  You, who are now overtaxed and declassed,
Laugh while you can, for the time may come round
  When the rubbish *you* treasure will lie in this place –
Your wireless set (bust), your ridiculous hats,
  The photographs of your period face.
Your best-selling novels, your 'functional' chairs,
  Your primitive comforts and notions of style
Are just so much fodder for dealers in junk –
  Let us hope that they'll make your grandchildren smile.

THE PLAYBOY OF THE DEMI-WORLD: 1938

Aloft in Heavenly Mansions, Doubleyou One –
Just Mayfair flats, but certainly sublime –
You'll find the abode of D'Arcy Honeybunn,
A rose-red sissy half as old as time.

Peace cannot age him, and no war could kill
The genial tenant of those cosy rooms,
He's lived there always and he lives there still,
Perennial pansy, hardiest of blooms.

There you'll encounter aunts of either sex,
Their jokes equivocal or over-ripe,
Ambiguous couples wearing slacks and specs
And the stout Lesbian knocking out her pipe.

The rooms are crammed with flowers and objets d'art,
A Ganymede still hands the drinks – and plenty!
D'Arcy still keeps a rakish-looking car
And still behaves the way he did at twenty.

A ruby pin is fastened in his tie,
The scent he uses is *Adieu Sagesse*,
His shoes are suède, and as the years go by
His tailor's bill's not getting any less.

He cannot whistle, always rises late,
Is good at indoor sports and parlour tricks,
Mauve is his favourite colour, and his gait
Suggests a peahen walking on hot bricks.

He prances forward with his hands outspread
And folds all comers in a gay embrace,
A wavy toupee on his hairless head,
A fixed smile on his often-lifted face.

'My dear!' he lisps, to whom all men are dear,
'How perfectly enchanting of you!'; turns
Towards his guests and twitters, 'Look who's here!
Do come and help us fiddle while Rome burns!'

'The kindest man alive,' so people say,
'Perpetual youth!' But have you seen his eyes?
The eyes of some old saurian in decay,
That asks no questions and is told no lies.

Under the fribble lurks a worn-out sage
Heavy with disillusion, and alone;
So never say to D'Arcy, 'Be your age!' –
He'd shrivel up at once or turn to stone.

FATHER AND SON: 1939

A family portrait not too stale to record
Of a pleasant old buffer, nephew to a lord,
Who believed that the bank was mightier than the sword,
And that an umbrella might pacify barbarians abroad:
>   Just like an old liberal
>   Between the wars.

With an easy existence, and a cosy country place,
And with hardly a wrinkle, at sixty, in his face,
Growing old with old books, with old wine, and with grace,
Unaware that events move at a breakneck pace:
>   Just like an old diehard
>   Between the wars.

With innocuous tastes in common with his mate,
A love of his garden and his tidy snug estate,
Of dogs, music and children, and lying in bed late,
And no disposition to quarrel with his fate:
>   Just like an old Englishman
>   Between the wars.

With no religion or imagination, and a hazy lazy view
Of the great world where trouble kept cropping up anew,
With old clubmen for friends, who would seem stuffy to you,
Old faded prigs, but gentlemen (give them their due):
>   Just like an old fossil
>   Between the wars.

With a kindly old wife who subscribed for the oppressed,
With an O.B.E., and hair-do like a last year's bird's nest,
Even more tolerant than anyone would have guessed,
Who hoped that in the long run all was for the best:
>   Just like an old lady
>   Between the wars.

With one child, a son, who in spite of his education
Showed only a modicum of common sense or cultivation,
Sometimes read the *Daily Worker* or the *New Statesman and Nation*,
But neither, it must be admitted, with much concentration:
> Just like a young playboy
> Between the wars.

With a firm grasp of half-truths, with political short-sight,
With a belief we could disarm but at the same time fight,
And that only the Left Wing could ever be right,
And that Moscow, of all places, was the sole source of light:
> Just like a young hopeful
> Between the wars.

With a flash flat in Chelsea of a bogus elegance,
With surrealist pictures and books puffed by Gollancz,
With a degree of complacence which nothing could enhance,
And without one sole well-wisher to kick him in the pants:
> Just like a young smarty
> Between the wars.

With a precious mistress who thought she could paint
But could neither show respect nor exercise restraint,
Was a perfect goose-cap, and thought good manners quaint,
With affectation enough to try the patience of a saint:
> Just like a young cutie
> Between the wars.

With a succession of parties for sponges and bores,
With a traffic-jam outside (for they turned up in scores),
With first-rate sherry flowing into second-rate whores,
And third-rate conversation without one single pause:
> Just like a young couple
> Between the wars.

With week ends in the country and holidays in France,
With promiscuous habits, time to sunbathe and dance,

And even to write books that were hardly worth a glance,
Earning neither reputation nor the publisher's advance:
> Just like a young writer
> Between the wars.

On a Sunday in September other troubles had begun,
There was argument at lunch between the father and the son,
Smoke rose from Warsaw and the beef was underdone,
Nothing points to heaven now but the anti-aircraft gun:
> With a hey nonny nonny
> And a hi-de-ho.

Oh, the 'twenties and the 'thirties were not otherwise designed
Than other times when blind men into ditches led the blind,
When the rich mouse ate the cheese and the poor mouse got the
    rind,
And man, the self-destroyer, was not lucid in his mind:
> With a hey nonny nonny
> And a hi-de-ho.

SLIGHTLY FOXED:
or, THE WIDOWER OF BAYSWATER

Decades ago wits, poets and dukes
Circled like planets round Gloria Jukes,
Bluestocking, tuft-hunter, *grande amoureuse* –
Was ever a *salon* brilliant as hers?

Her name still turns up though she's turned up her toes,
You meet her in memoirs, they still quote her *mots*,
And old crones remember her faults and her furs –
Such foibles, my dear, such sables were hers!

A wrecker of homes and a breaker of hearts
She talked like a book and encouraged the arts,
Political hostesses envied her poise,
And said they preferred conversation to noise.

Her cook was a dream, her pearls were in ropes,
She furthered ambitions, she realized hopes,
Lent Dowson a fiver, put rouge on her eyebrows,
Enchanted grandees and reconciled highbrows.

Acclimatized novel Bohemian behaviour
In the stuffiest house in Victorian Belgravia,
And when St John's Wood was abandoned to orgies
Behaved like a dignified bride at St George's.

A Personage paid to her regal *poitrine*
A compliment royal, and she looked like a queen –
But of some Ruritanian kingdom, maybe –
All plastered with gifts like a Christmas tree.

When her guests were awash with champagne and with gin
She was recklessly sober, as sharp as a pin:
An abstemious man would reel at her look
As she rolled a bright eye and praised his last book.

She twitted George Moore, she flirted with Tree,
Gave dear Rider Haggard material for *She*,
Talked scansion with Bridges and scandal with Wilde,
To Drinkwater drank and Crackanthorpe smiled.

Brzeska and Brooke were among those she knew,
And she lived long enough to meet Lawrences too,
D.H. and T.E. – she, who'd known R.L.S.,
Talked to Hardy of *Kim*, and to Kipling of *Tess*!

Now she's been dead for more than ten years
We look round in vain to discover her peers;
The Gloria (it has often been said) is departed
And a new, and inferior period has started ...

But tucked right away in a Bayswater attic,
Arthritic, ignoble, stone-deaf and rheumatic,
There still lingers on, by the strangest of flukes,
Yes, Gloria's husband – Plantagenet Jukes!

Ignored in her lifetime, he paid for her fun,
And enjoyed all the fuss. When she died he was done.
He sold up the house and retired from the scene
Where nobody noticed that he'd ever been.

His memoirs unwritten (though once he began 'em)
He lives on a hundred and fifty per annum
And once in the day totters out for a stroll
To purchase two eggs, *The Times*, and a roll.

Up to now he has paid for his pleasures and needs
With books he had saved and that everyone reads,
Signed copies presented by authors to Gloria
In the reigns of King Edward and good Queen Victoria.

They brought in fair prices but came to an end,
Then Jukes was reduced to one book-loving friend,
A girl of the streets with a smatter of culture
And the genial ways of an African vulture.

125

To this bird he offered the last of the lot,
A volume of Flecker beginning to rot.
She opened it, stormed: 'Cor blimey, you're potty!
D'you think I can't see that the pages are spotty!

'Your Flecker is foxed, you old fool, and I'm through!'
Then out of the door in a tantrum she flew,
Leaving poor Jukes, in the black-out, in bed
With his past, and the book, and a bruise on his head.

NIGHT THOUGHTS IN THE
TOTTENHAM COURT ROAD: 1942

There were things we never saw when
    Noisy peace lit up the road,
Cornices in decent darkness,
    Cupolas that never showed.

Like an actress in the limelight,
    Ageing and no longer starred,
Frightful now in chalky moonlight
    Looms a 1910 façade.

Tarnished each mosaic and moulding –
    Even new they were debased;
All her ornaments are tawdry –
    Even young she was not chaste;

On the street this many a year, she
    Never caught the eye before,
Tall and livid, the old stager
    Takes advantage of the war;

Takes advantage of the black-out
    To array herself in white
And affront with all her detail
    Heaven, April and the night.

Thus are whims of building fathers
    Visited in moonlit air
On the children, whose false teeth are
    Set on edge by *laissez-faire* ...

Yet, as we gaze, we come to love her,
    Wondering if future years
Will allow for freaks and folly
    And the nonsense that endears.

Slaves to what is merely useful,
    Uniform and up-to-date,
We may long for what's capricious,
    Fanciful, unique, ornate –

So, old girl we now salute you
    Though at first your make-up jarred:
Long life to your flat pilasters!
    Bouquets to your odd façade!

THE FLYING BUM: 1944

In the vegetarian guest-house
All was frolic, feast and fun,
Eager voices were enquiring
'Are the nettle cutlets done?'
Peals of vegetarian laughter,
Husky wholesome wholemeal bread,
Will the evening finish with a
Rush of cocoa to the head?

Yes, you've guessed; it's Minnie's birthday,
Hence the frolic, hence the feast.
Are there calories in custard?
There are vitamins in yeast.
Kate is here and Tom her hubby,
Ex-commissioner for oaths,
She is mad on Christian Science,
Parsnip flan he simply loathes.

And Mr Croaker, call him Arthur,
Such a keen philatelist,
Making sheep's-eyes at Louisa
(After dinner there'll be whist) –
Come, sit down, the soup is coming,
All of docks and darnels made,
Drink a health to dear old Minnie
In synthetic lemonade.

Dentures champing juicy lettuce,
Champing macerated bran,
Oh the imitation rissoles!
Oh the food untouched by man!
Look, an imitation sausage
Made of monkey-nuts and spice,
Prunes tonight and semolina,
Wrinkled prunes, unpolished rice.

Yards of guts absorbing jellies,
Bellies filling up with nuts,
Carbohydrates jostling proteins
Out of intestinal ruts;
Peristalsis calls for roughage,
Haulms and fibres, husks and grit,
Nature's way to open bowels,
Maybe – let them practise it.

'Hark, I hear an air-raid warning!'
'Take no notice, let 'em come.'
'Who'll say grace?' 'Another walnut?'
'Listen, what's that distant hum?'
'Bomb or no bomb,' stated Minnie,
'Lips unsoiled by beef or beer
We shall use to greet our Maker
When he sounds the Great All-Clear.'

When the flying bomb exploded
Minnie's wig flew off her pate,
Half a curtain, like a tippet,
Wrapped itself round bony Kate,
Plaster landed on Louisa,
Tom fell headlong on the floor,
And a spurt of lukewarm custard
Lathered Mr Croaker's jaw.

All were spared by glass and splinters
But, the loud explosion past,
Greater was the shock impending
Even than the shock of blast –
Blast we veterans know as freakish
Gave this feast its final course,
Planted bang upon the table
A lightly roasted rump of horse.

A SHOT IN THE PARK

[Based upon an incident in the memoirs of the Edwardian hostess, Mrs Hwfa Williams.]

1

In the light beneath the leafage
In the afternoon in May
In the Park and near the Row
Gracefully from Hwfa*
Mrs Hwfa Williams turned away,
Saying 'Hwfa, I must go,
I expect a mob for tea;
Such fun, but I must fly –
You dine, I think with me?
Till then, my dear, good-bye!'

Mrs Hwfa Williams
Twirled and furled her parasol,
Lightly stepped into her carriage,
Thinking it was all such fun –
Life, and May, and marriage.
Such a pretty moment –
How were they to figure
Fate in ambush, taking aim,
Finger on the trigger?

Later in a tea-gown talking
Over twinkling tea-things on a tray
(Hwfa in the Park still walking)
She was heard to say:

'When my husband and I gave it out
We should move to Great Cumberland Place
My sister-in-law gave a shriek –
"My dears, you'll be lost without trace!"
    And she said it with such a grimace!

* Pronounce *Hoover*.

130

'"It's so utterly out of the world!
So fearfully wide of the mark!
A Robinson Crusoe existence will pall
On that unexplored side of the Park –
    Not a soul will be likely to call!"

'Disparaging all one adores,
Relations are such a disgrace;
They gossip, as bluebottles buzz,
They deplore what one is and one does –
    But they call at Great Cumberland Place!'

2

At home the tea-time tittle-tattle; in the Mall
Two different orbits about to intersect:
That a poor clerk and Mr Hwfa Williams
Should there converge nobody could expect
And only a clairvoyant could foretell.

Gravely conferring with a crony, Hwfa
On one side saunters; on the other glares
A young man, seemingly a loafer,
Whose small brain, infinitely busier than theirs,
Has been inflamed by Post Office affairs.

He sends the telegrams that other people write;
From overwork a breakdown now impends;
Abrupt, elliptic phrases day and night he sends,
Recurring in his fevered brain all day
To be reiterated in his brain all night.

Now all's confused, things are not what they seem,
He stands bemused, as if he had been drinking;
Life is a cryptic, an intolerable dream –
RETURN TONIGHT AUNT HENRIETTA SINKING:
CONGRATULATIONS DEAR FROM ALL AT CHEAM.
GLOXINIA WILTING ORDER PINK GERANIUM:

TEN THOUSAND OFFERED SILLY NOT TO SELL:
Telegraphese tattoos upon his eardrums,
Like red-hot tintacks drives into his cranium
The public syntax of his private hell –

THANK YOU BOTH ENCHANTED:
OIL CONCESSION GRANTED:
HOPE ARRIVE NUNEATON TEN TO EIGHT:
ARRIVING SEVEN MABEL STOP:
DON'T SELL REFECTORY TABLE STOP:
CAT OUT OF BAG YOUR TELEGRAM TOO LATE.

Suddenly he sees two frock-coats passing,
Two top-hats tilted in tête-à-tête –
These are to blame! Revenge upon the senders
Of countless telegrams! He feels the uprush
Of a delayed explosive charge of hate.

He draws and points a pistol, then he shoots.
'Ouch!' cries Hwfa. Something has distressed him.
He stumbles, mutters 'Somebody has shot me!'
He falls. Blood falls upon his patent-leather boots,
And cries go up, 'A murderer! Arrest him!'

3

In the light beneath the leafage
Late that afternoon in May,
In the Mall and on the ground
Mr Hwfa Williams lay,
Happily not dead, but wounded.

'How do you feel?' they asked.
'Injured,' he said, 'and quite astounded.'

Mr Hwfa Williams
Was attended by a Dr Fletcher,
And vexed, but bravely bland,
Was carried home upon a stretcher;

132

And
On Mr Hwfa Williams' forehead
Mrs Hwfa Williams laid a
Ministering angel's hand.

Later 'Hwfa,' Mrs Hwfa Williams said,
'Do you prefer the sofa to your bed?'

'My dear, I don't mind *where* I lie;
What *does* it signify
When not a living soul can tell me why,
About to cross St James's Park
I'm picked on like a sitting pheasant
By, so they tell me, a demented clerk,
A truant from the G.P.O., Mount Pleasant?
Too many wires, they say, had turned his brain –
But why he turned on *me* – no, *that* they can't explain.'

4

'Good morning, have you heard the news?
You'll be amazed!' 'Well, what?'
'I nearly fainted when I read
That Hwfa Williams has been shot.'

'My dear, your coffee's getting cold – '
'Well, does it matter in the least?'
All over London in the morning
Breakfast was a headline feast.

'Now here is what the paper says:
*A dastardly assault ... the crime
Seems without motive ... an arrest was made ...
Alleged ... admitted ... passing at the time ...*

'*A grudge ... dispatch of telegrams ...
Pistol discarded, lying in the mud ...
Enquiries made at Mr Williams' home ...
Life not in danger ... shock and loss of blood.*

133

'No one is safe, it seems, these days:
To stroll across St James's Park
Is to receive a bullet in the leg
From some unhinged, ferocious clerk:

'A little learning, as our fathers knew,
Is certainly a dangerous thing;
The lower orders have been spoilt,
And now they mean to have their fling;

'But though the world's all upside down
And England hastening to decay,
Ring for the carriage; we'll enquire
How Hwfa Williams is today.'

5

'Crikey!' said the butler, Crichton,
'Blocking up the blooming street
All these callers keep on calling –
No one thinks of my poor feet!

'All the toffs with all their questions,
Leaving cards you can't refuse;
These reporters, nosy parkers,
Proper sharks they are for news.

'I was not engaged to answer
Bells that jangle all the time,
These enquiries well might drive a
Better man than me to crime:

'*How's your master? Is he better?*
Is his life in danger still?
Is it true a gang attacked him?
Do you think they shot to kill?

'*Can you tell us why they did it?*
Anarchists? A Fenian plot?
More of this and I'll go barmy,
Like the lad that fired the shot.'

Carriage after carriage crowding,
Kind enquirers choke the street:
How is Mr Hwfa Williams?
'No one thinks of MY POOR FEET!'

6

'And so,' said Mrs Hwfa Williams,
Telling the story after years had passed,
'It seemed that half of London came to call.
Fruit, game and flowers came crowding thick and fast,
Cards like confetti rained into the hall –
Such a great fuss, poor Hwfa was aghast
Yet pleased, I think, at such extreme concern,
More pleased than our old butler with it all –
Poor Crichton hardly knew which way to turn.

'The street was jammed, the knocker and the bell
Clamoured together like two fiends in hell –
And where was Crichton? Nobody could tell!
At twelve o'clock my maid rushed in and said
"Oh, ma'am, he's drinking quarts of brandy neat –
Crichton's gone mad! I'll see to the front door!"
Not mad but drunk I found him. Bursting into song
With "Home Sweet Home", he lurched and hit the floor.
'Abject when sober, Crichton said his feet
Had driven him off his head, nor had he known
That Hwfa's best old brandy was so strong ...
Hwfa forgave him, he had been with us so long.

'He stayed for years ... Poor man, his race is run ...
I also soon shall hear the sunset gun –
But in between times life has been *such fun*!'

135

COUNTRY BALLADS AND POEMS

RURAL SPORT

Workmen digging in the park
The other afternoon
Turned up a skull – an excuse
To knock off work too soon.

'Prop it up there, and watch me,
I'll make the baldy skip!'
So they varied a dull hot day
With loutish marksmanship.

Better than darts it was
To pelt this comic mark
The marl had sepulchred
For ages, for them, for a lark.

They smashed it all to bits,
Death's image, a Roman head,
While the new landlord lay
At the Hall, in sickbed,

One of these scientists –
'If only I'd known,' he said,
'I'd have given them pounds,
I'd have given my head

'For that skull they destroyed:
It seems that schools
And wireless have not yet shown
Their folly to fools.'

If only they too had known!
They weren't half sick,
And believed that the skull itself
Had played them a trick.

DECEMBER AT LINGEN

A ladder in the orchard, and a handsaw hisses
Where a small summer in bare boughs these weeks has hung,
The saw of John Davies rasping dry twigs among
To sever the mistletoe, bouquets of olive-green sprays
Prolific with pale pearls and a promise of kisses.

Springy the burden, the rustling bower of sprays
Returning he brings from the apple-tree garth,
Trousers and coat green-stained, along the moss-deep path,
Alone along the path by which his happiness went,
Shamefaced, jilted Davies, plodding along intent
With heavy step and solid jowl through the frosty mist –
And a mouth for each mistletoe-pearl will kiss and be kissed.

NEW LEAVES

Through stone arch foaming
And strained through saplings
The flooded stream
In full stress
Flows by the ruin,
The castle ruin
In the owl-haunted, rain-lonely
Bracken mountain.

Within these walls,
Grass-tufted, ivy-curtained
Roofless walls,
The stonebreaker's son
With a branch of spindleberries
Points to the crinkly
Tiny-puckered
Fresh green primrose leaves
Pushing through leaf-mould.

Unforgettable gesture!
So was the Zulu's
Throwing red earth
From a grassy grave;
And the Polish hussar's
Whose fine hand
Unslung his cloak,
His braided cloak;
And the Chinese woman's
Using the telephone
For the second time;
And the Greek's who sighed
(So far from Wales
And this rainy ruin)
One night of love
In rocky, thymy,
Dry bright Attica.

THE MURDER ON THE DOWNS

Past a cow and past a cottage,
Past the sties and byres,
Past the equidistant poles
Holding taut the humming wires,

Past the inn and past the garage,
Past the hypodermic steeple
Ever ready to inject
The opium of the people,

In the fresh, the Sussex morning,
Up the Dangerous Corner lane
Bert and Jennifer were walking
Once again.

The spider's usual crochet
Was caught upon the thorns,
The skylark did its stuff,
The cows had horns.

'See,' said Bert, 'my hand is sweating.'
With her lips she touched his palm
As they took the path above the
Valley farm.

Over the downs the wind unveiled
That ancient monument the sun,
And a perfect morning
Had begun.

But summer lightning like an omen
Carried on a silent dance
On his heart's horizon, as he
Gave a glance

At the face beside him, and she turned
Dissolving in his frank blue eyes
All her hope, like aspirin.
On that breeding-place of lies

His forehead, too, she laid her lips.
'Let's find a place to sit,' he said.
'Past the gorse, down in the bracken
Like a bed.'

Oh the fresh, the laughing morning!
Warmth upon the bramble brake
Like a magnet draws from darkness
A reviving snake:

Just an adder, slowly gliding,
Sleepy curving idleness,
On the Sussex turf now writing
SOS.

Jennifer in sitting, touches
With her hand an agaric,
Like a bulb of rotten rubber
Soft and thick,

Screams, withdraws, and sees its colour
Like a leper's liver,
Leans on Bert so he can feel her
Shiver.

Over there the morning ocean,
Frayed around the edges, sighs,
At the same time gaily twinkles,
Conniving with a million eyes

At Bert whose free hand slowly pulls
A rayon stocking from his coat,
Twists it quickly, twists it neatly,
Round her throat.

'Ah, I knew that this would happen!'
Her last words: and not displeased
Jennifer relaxed, still smiling
While he squeezed.

Under a sky without a cloud
Lay the still unruffled sea,
And in the bracken like a bed
The murderee.

THE DORKING THIGH

About to marry and invest
Their lives in safety and routine
Stanley and June required a nest
And came down on the 4.15.

The agent drove them to the Posh Estate
And showed them several habitations.
None did. The afternoon got late
With questions, doubts, and explanations.

Then day grew dim and Stan fatigued
And disappointment raised its head,
But June declared herself intrigued
To know where that last turning led.

It led to a Tudor snuggery styled
'Ye Kumfi Nooklet' on the gate.
'A gem of a home,' the salesman smiled,
'My pet place on the whole estate;

'It's not quite finished, but you'll see
Good taste itself.' They went inside.
'This little place is built to be
A husband's joy, a housewife's pride.'

144

They saw the white convenient sink,
The modernistic chimneypiece,
June gasped for joy, Stan gave a wink
To say, 'Well, here our quest can cease.'

The salesman purred (he'd managed well)
And June undid a cupboard door.
'For linen,' she beamed. And out there fell
A nameless Something on the floor.

'Something the workmen left, I expect.'
The agent said, as it fell at his feet,
Nor knew that his chance of a sale was wrecked.
'Good heavens, it must be a joint of meat!'

Ah yes, it was meat, it was meat all right,
A joint those three will never forget –
For they stood alone in the Surrey night
With the severed thigh of a plump brunette ...

*   *   *

Early and late, early and late,
Traffic was jammed round the Posh Estate,
And the papers were full of the Dorking Thigh
And who, and when, and where, and why.

A trouser button was found in the mud.
(Who made it? Who wore it? Who lost it? Who knows?)
But no one found a trace of blood
Or her body or face, or the spoiler of those.

He's acting a play in the common air
On which no curtain can ever come down.
Though 'Ye Kumfi Nooklet' was shifted elsewhere
June made Stan take a flat in town.

THE BUNGALOWS

In lofty light the towers dissolve
Of yellow elms this tranquil day,
Crumble in leisurely showers of gold
All Turneresque in bright decay.

The elms disperse their leaves upon
A nineteen-thirty builder's row
Of speculative dwellings, each
An unassuming bungalow.

Like concave shells, or shades, or shields
That guard some life or light aloof,
Like hands that cup a flame, or keep
Some frail and captured thing, each roof.

If high-pitched hopes have gone to roost
Where low-pitched roofs so smoothly slope
Perhaps these autumn rays diffuse
A deeper anodyne than hope.

Between the vast insanities
That men so cleverly invent
It may be here, it may be here,
A simulacrum of content.

Though separate only from the road
By five-foot hedge and ten-foot lawn
Each semi-isolationist
Seems almost from the world withdrawn,

Except that from a roof or two
Those thin and wand-like aerials rise
That suck like opium from the air
Bemusement for the ears and eyes.

146

The denizens of each hermitage,
Of 'Nellibert' and 'Mirzapore',
Bird-watchers all, in love with dogs,
Are primed with useful garden-lore:

Cabbage the emblem of their life –
Yet mauve the michaelmas-daisy glows
And under reddening apples gleams
A pearly, pure, belated rose.

Begrudging vulgar fantasy
To cheap and ordinary homes,
Discrimination might deplore
That concrete frog, those whimsy gnomes,

Nor see them as blind tribute to
The rule of dreams, or as a last
Concession to the irrational,
The old, wild, superstitious past.

The commonplace needs no defence,
Dullness is in the critic's eyes,
Without a licence life evolves
From some dim phase its own surprise:

Under these yellow-twinkling elms,
Behind these hedges trimly shorn,
As in a stable once, so here
It may be born, it may be born.

ATHELING GRANGE:
or, THE APOTHEOSIS OF LOTTE NUSSBAUM

[From a Sussex newspaper, October, 1953: 'HOUSEKEEPER MISSING –
Miss Lotte Nussbaum (48), who came to this country as a refugee from Nazi
Germany before the war, is reported missing from Spindrift, Hydrangea-avenue,
Atheling-on-Sea, where she has for some years resided as housekeeper to Mrs
Elvaston-Clunch.

'As Miss Nussbaum's shopping-basket is also missing, it is thought that she
may have gone out to gather blackberries or mushrooms, and may be suffering
from loss of memory. Search parties have failed to find any trace of the missing
woman.']

1

A heavy mist. A muffled sea.
A cloth of cobwebs veils the grass.
Upstairs alone the refugee
   Sees autumn in her glass:

A touch of autumn in the air,
The knife of autumn in the heart
Of one too constantly aware
   Of living half apart.

Is comfort peace? Can it restore
The severed root within the mind?
Domestic service evermore
   Is not what hope designed:

Kindly and rich and not a fool
The widow whom she housekeeps for,
But unadventurous, so cool,
   So English, such a bore.

Today the harmless Mrs Clunch
Went up to London on her own,
And Lotte, dreamy after lunch,
   Feels even more alone:

148

She has no one to whom to turn
And reminisce of those lost lives
The autumn smell of leaf and fern
   So poignantly revives;

It quickens an old appetite,
This dank and thrilling smell;
She feels a craving now to bite
   Mushroom or Chanterelle;

Off with a basket she will go
To find if, where the fields begin,
Some palatable fungi grow,
   And if so, bring them in;

She knows the very ones to look for –
Fresh, firm, not too mature –
There'll only be herself to cook for,
   A secret epicure!

2

Lotte acquired upon her native hills
   The caution of a fungivore,
Knew how to look a *Giftpilz* in the gills
And where for *Steinpilz* one had best explore,
So now with confidence she reconnoitres,
Steps forward, backward, stoops, intently loiters.

Though no mycophagist could be more eager,
   She finds she isn't doing well,
After an hour her harvesting is meagre –
Two Puffballs, and a not too fresh Morel;
But strolling on beyond her usual range
She comes to the deserted Atheling Grange.

149

3

Where formerly curlews were calling
And orchises fell with the hay
The last of the meadows are falling
To bungalows gnawing their way;

The seaboard is doubly eroded –
To seaward by gale-driven water,
And inland, where fields are outmoded
By inroads of bricks and of mortar;

But still, though its owners have died out,
An island of ilex encloses
A nineteenth-century hide-out
Once lovely with lawns and with roses;

The owls, who succeeded its owners,
Would quit it with screeches tonight
If they knew that the place is now known as
A 'ripe-for-development' site.

The state of the place is appalling –
What is wrongly described as a shambles;
Everywhere ivy is crawling
And striving to strangle the brambles;

Everywhere brambles are clinging
And creepers are climbing and creeping,
The nettles are ready for stinging,
The willows have reason for weeping;

The woods were cut down in the 'twenties,
The farm was sold off at a loss,
The lodge is kept only by woodlice,
The gateposts are padded with moss;

Bindweed has smothered the greenhouse,
The summer-house under the yew
Is now just a cannot-be-seen house
That commands an invisible view.

O house once delightfully lived in,
O Atheling Grange, did they build you
For dry rot and wet rot to feed on,
A medium for mould and for mildew?

Why ask such an imbecile question?
That rhetorical style has gone by,
And nothing would be more surprising
Than to hear the old ruin reply.

With bunches of bats on the ceilings
And droppings of rats in the hall,
The decline of the Grange is complete and
At any time now it may fall.

4

Though Lotte is aware how torn her coat is,
    Full steam ahead she ploughs and pushes
Tank-like through snags and tangled thorny bushes,
Quite undeterred by wire or warning notice,
Convinced this *Hintergarten* she has found
Will prove to be her happy hunting-ground.

How right she is – but God knows how she knew it!
    She's in a mycophil's Utopia
Where autumn, from a golden cornucopia,
Has tipped out every sort of Cèpe and Blewit.
She fills her basket quickly. New to her
Truffles one doesn't have to disinter;

Not new to her, but never yet so keen,
    So *appetitlich* and so rich
That mushroom smell; nor has she ever seen

151

The Beefsteak Fungus growing in a ditch;
Here on a stump some tender Buff Caps quiver,
There Pluteus swells, like Strasburg goose's liver;

And peering downward through a rusty grating
    Into what used to be the cellars
She sees there, prettily proliferating,
A multitude of little beige umbrellas,
Throngs of a choice and edible Boletus
That seem to say 'Come down, my dear, and eat us!'

'*Embarras de richesse!*' she might exclaim,
    If she could coin so French a phrase –
So many kinds she doesn't know by name,
All ready to be cooked in different ways:
But who to feed? She yearns to summon up
Her long-lost kin to sit with her and sup.

'*Himmel!*' she sighs ... And at that very word
    Celestial choirs inflate the breeze,
Die ganze Vogelschar gets busy in the trees,
And then a band – a German band – is heard
Playing a waltz by Waldteufel or Strauss,
And all the lights light up inside the house.

'*Himmel!*' she cries. And so it is – she's right!
    Across the new-mown lawn advance
Her long-lost family, arrayed in white,
Her parents leading in a lively dance
Her brothers, sisters, nieces, uncles, aunts,
With crowns and harps – a most unearthly sight!

Oh, what a welcome for Miss Nussbaum! See,
    All's *himmelhoch* and *himmelblau*!
Heaven is hers, and she is Heaven's now!
She's disembodied, disencumbered, free!
Lotte is free! ... Tomorrow Mrs Clunch
Will have no drudge to cook her bla sted lunch.

THE PALMER TRIPLETS

['At an old house near the Decoy, now converted into cottages ... lived,
in the reign of Henry VIII, Lady Palmer, the famous mother of the Palmer
triplets, who were distinguished from other triplets, not only by being born each
on a successive Sunday but by receiving each the honour of knighthood. The
curious circumstances of their birth seem to be well attested.' E. V. Lucas:
Highways and Byways in Sussex.]

1. *Nineteenth Century*

Smoke from a chimney lazed
   (Seen in an old vignette);
'Dream and remember,' wrote the smoke,
   'Or waken and forget';

Jotted against a cloud
   A spray of v-shaped birds
Spelt in their static formation-flight
   A message without words;

Summer was in the cloud
   And the heavy cumulus trees,
The drum of the sun-warmed ear was lulled
   By undertones of bees;

A crone with a load of wood
   Resting beside the road
Drugged with the obsolete afternoon
   Dozed by the old abode;

The stump of the courtly house
   Stood firm, the hag was bent
In a courtesy to approaching death,
   A bow that was permanent:

Peace like a coma shut
   The scene, that house, her bow,
From the great fine worrying world
   (As raging then as now);

153

Peace in the dormant house –
    Ah, but a puzzling thing,
The caption in Gothic script beneath
    Said 𝔑𝔢𝔴 𝔓𝔩𝔞𝔠𝔢, 𝔄𝔱𝔥𝔢𝔩𝔦𝔫𝔤.

How was it ever new
    This place imbued with age
An age before that view was drawn
    For an Early Victorian page?

2. *Sixteenth Century*

For the long journey out of Kent new-dressed
In a white mantle with a fur-trimmed hood
Four hundred years ago at New Place stood
Sir Edward Palmer's bride; she stood stock-still,
Stared at the bold-emblazoned Palmer crest
And felt a strange surrender of the will.

Heraldic art in images proclaims
The worship of fertility and blood.
The Palmer totem, from the herald's stud,
Was half a panther, argent and irate,
And issuant from its eager head were flames
All proper, as from a domestic grate.

Alice, confronted with the panther, felt
Its teeth and flame-red breath and silver pelt
More than symbolic of her husband's race:
Its rampant beauty seemed to glorify
His new-found image in her inward eye,
Their love's ferocious joy and feral grace.

New Place, new wife, new Lady Palmer: married,
She found a promise in that gonfalon
And in the palm-branch that the panther carried –
Promise of victory in life's long war,
Promise of life, with peace to follow on.
She turned, she smiled, her diffidence all gone.

154

Famous in history and obstetric lore
The Palmer triplets. On a Sunday one
Was born; after a week a second son:
They say a woman's work is never done –
In labour still, Sir Edward's lady bore
On the third Sunday safely one son more.

'My loving pride has equally been shared
Between my sons,' their ageing dam declared,
'My three bright panthers of a single litter –
Sir John, Sir Henry, and Sir Thomas Palmer,
Each son a champion and not one a quitter,
Each a stout stuffing for a suit of armour.

'Henry the Eighth gave each the accolade
In turn for valour. My son John survives,
But two in earth, God rest their souls, are laid –
God rest them, they were valiant in their lives.
Henry died old in battle for this nation,
Tom was beheaded – for miscalculation.

'My babes arrived without unseemly haste,
With health and strength all three by God were graced;
Myself like them must soon be laid in earth
But may be not forgotten in this land
(Old doddering dowager now with shaking hand)
Because of their unprecedented birth.'

3. *Twentieth Century*

The stump of the aged house
    Remains exactly yet
As the graver saw it who set himself
    To devise a new vignette.

Passing the old Decoy
    Look ahead through the thick
Upstart rods of elder and ash
    At the warm and rosy brick;

155

The chimney is still the same,
  Smoke rises, fire still warms,
But life takes on in the Tudor rooms
  New, un-Tudor forms;

Under the apple-trees
  Slacks hung up to dry
In a casual can-can slackly kick
  Towards the same old sky;

They seem to be keeping time
  To something on 'the Light':
The cowman's daughter's boy-friend goes
  With her to a dance tonight;

On the back of his motor-bike
  They're off to a Gala Hop,
She'll wear her apricot nylon dress,
  Her shoes from the Co-op.

Good luck to you, girl, with your new,
  Your healthy Sussex face,
And, boy, to you: and come back safe
  To this far from new New Place.

Though the panther-breed have moved
  To another sphere or shire,
A panther lurks in every heart –
  Beware, its breath is fire!

BAMBOO:
A BALLAD FOR TWO VOICES

1

SHE: However dry and windless
        Cold days, hot nights may be,
        Bamboo, incessant rustler,
        Your restless leafage utters
        A sound of wind and rain:
        Nobody knows the nervous
        Effect it has on me –
        I cannot stand the strain,
        Bamboo, I cannot stand it,
        Your whispering campaign!

HE: I love, bamboo, your fidgets
        And sudden sighs, bamboo;
        Awake alone I listen
        To secret susurration
        Like paper scraping stone;
        Stroking the inner surface
        Of this old heart, bamboo,
        Whisper to me alone
        Your wordless reminiscence –
        And resurrect my own!

SHE: Here is the explanation
        Why what he loves I hate:
        My husband was a sailor
        Out on the China Station –
        (If I had known him then!
        It seems the best life offers
        Is second-best, and late;
        Unsure of *what* and *when*
        A girl may miss her chances –
        What did I know of men?)

157

The girl he'll never talk of
And never can forget
Has always come between us:
I see her sly and slant-eyed
Haunting some furtive wood,
Slender in silk, and artful;
The moment that they met
Her doubtful maidenhood
Pleased him beyond all reason –
She stole his heart for good.

Before I ever knew him
The dew, the down, the bloom
Were brushed away in Asia –
Hers was his startling April,
His wildfire blossoming.
The years of humdrum fondness,
The habit-forming room
Are quite another thing –
I hate her for devouring
His unrecurring spring!

HE: Her skin was like a primrose,
In sheets of silk her feet
Slender as sleeping finches
Slept while the snow was heaping
A feather barricade
Between us and the future:
At first, so sly and sweet,
It seemed an escapade,
But we were caught together –
Love caught us while we played.

I felt her small heart racing,
Quick heart imprisoned in
Her flexile, bird-boned body,
As if another being
Conscious that it was mute

Beat desperate, beat lonely,
Against the screen of skin:
The hot moon smelt of fruit,
Looming up huge to listen
To one thin bamboo flute.

And that is why I planted
A thicket of bamboo
Here is an English garden –
Waving bamboo was witness
Of all that love can be:
I live at home and listen,
And you revive, bamboo,
After a life at sea,
The only overwhelming
Love ever shown to me.

SHE :   How I dislike the supple
         Canes, and the harsh coarse leaves!
         There's something so suburban
         About bamboos.

HE :   The waving
         Bamboo recalls the sway
         Of young and fertile bodies
         And lifted, long, silk sleeves.

SHE :   Suburban, as I say.

HE :   The wordless reminiscence
         Is whispered night and day.

2

SHE :   Now that he's dead and buried
         At last, at last I'm free
         To make my chosen changes
         Put off when he was living:
         I'm captain now, and crew –

159

(No freedom like a widow's!) –
And who's to disagree
With what I mean to do?
Root, shoot, and stem and sucker,
I'll root out that bamboo!

HIS GHOST: (*softly, from a distance*)
That's what you think, old helpmate,
But always I shall swim
Along your psyche's courses,
The frogman in your bloodstream
You never can evade;
By cutting down that sappy
Bamboo you'd injure him
Whose peace of mind you made –
You know you'll never touch it
With secateurs or spade!

3

HIS GHOST: Bamboo, she used to hate you
But lonely now she hears
And half believes your voice is
Not yours but mine – ironic
That she discovers now
A soft association,
Even a source of tears,
In what she once described as
'A vicious rasping sound' –
It now puts her in mind of
Her husband underground.

SHE: Strange, that I used to hate you,
His keepsake plant, bamboo!
In solitude your sighings
Recall my old companion
And not his dreamt-of past.

HIS GHOST: We phantoms have our triumphs.

SHE: You're *my* plant now, bamboo!

HIS GHOST: She understands at last
Why I was pleased to hear you.

SHE: I understand at last.

HIS GHOST: Hush-hush those open secrets
You'll much rehearse alone
When we are both reduced to
Potential fertilizer
For plants like you, bamboo.

SHE: Two butterflies beside you
A moment on a stone –

HE: Would not be us, bamboo!
And now long life we wish you,
Long-loved, light-leaved bamboo.

HIS GHOST: ⎱ *(together, very softly)*
SHE: ⎰ Bamboo, bamboo, bamboo!

THE HEART OF A KING:

An Incident at Nuneham, 1856.

[Frances, Countess Waldegrave (1821–79), wife of George Granville Harcourt.
Dr William Buckland (1784–1856), formerly Dean of Westminster, Professor
of Mineralogy, and Reader in Geology at Oxford.]

1. *Before Dinner*

LADY WALDEGRAVE:
  I hope you will be pleased, your fellow-guest
  To-night will be Dean Buckland, such a dear,
  So doddery now, but brilliant at his best,
  He loves, I know, to be invited here.

  You've no idea how vast his knowledge is,
  And yet he's, oh, so modest all the same!
  THEO and GEO are the two chief OLOGIES
  In which he has made so great a name.

  A shade eccentric, but we must allow
  Great men their foibles – *I* think so, don't you?
  (I think it best to let you know this now
  In case of strange things he may say or do.)

  Over beaches trudging and across hills
  He used to hunt out every sort of stones,
  And in the pulpit, brandishing some fossils,
  Praised the Creator, and found sermons, yes, in *bones*.

  He'd find in mud a moral, and unravel
  God's purpose from a pebble, preach
  Sermons so full of grace and gravel
  My husband called them *lapidary* speech.

  But here he is! How are you, Mr Dean?
  How nice this is! We hope we see you well?

162

DR BUCKLAND:
Ah, *how*, dear lady, can I tell?
I'm not the man I've been,
No, not at all, not I!
Sometimes when I try
To step I stumble,
Try not to tumble –
Bad to tumble –
Mustn't slip or stumble.
Steps are so steep, and stones
Are slippery; and bones,
Old bones, are brittle; so are stones,
Some stones; don't want to break my bones
Like biscuits, want to make old bones,
Old broken bones don't mend.
I'm old, I can't pretend
I'm not. I stoop; I stumble
When I walk; and when I talk, I mumble;
And when I feel, I fumble;
And one more thing, I can't unbend,
And as I near my end
I find I tend,
Yes, more and more I tend
To grumble.

LADY WALDEGRAVE:
Oh, not at all, a younger man might covet
A quarter of your energy and charm,
The sight of you's a pleasure, and we love it –
But dinner is ready, may I take your arm?

2. *During Dinner*

DR BUCKLAND:
As I was going to say,
As I was thinking just the other day,
My memory's not as active as it was.
Since I was young (I *was* young, was I not?

163

I ask because my memory's not
As active as it was),
Since I was young, I say,
I've never tasted claret quite so choice –
It warms the memory and restores the voice.

Forgive me if I take, with your permission,
To being somewhat talkative –
I find good wine, uncorkative,
Drives me to reminiscion.

Dear Lady Waldegrave, do you know Lyme Regis?
I well remember a Miss Mary Anning
In Eighteen-Twenty-something, there beneath the aegis
Of her good father. One would see them scanning

Some curious formation. Carrying a box
For specimens, and the neatest little hammer,
She'd listen to his explanations of the rocks,
Just like a bright-eyed pupil with a crammer.

Then one day peering, just about as high as
Tiptoes allowed her, suddenly she saw
Embedded in a stratum of blue lias
A startling fossil never seen before.

Those wondrous bones, imagine, had been lying
By God's good providence preserved intact till
That very moment, ready for identifying
By me – how fortunate! – as the *Pterodactyl*!

To say our senses make the truest teachers
Seems rather pagan, does it not? But oh, by Jove,
Something (I hope due reverence for God's creatures)
Impelled me then to *taste* that treasure trove.

Since then I have always found a quick
Flick of the tongue enables me to test
The surfaces of substances – often a lick
Confirms what I had only guessed.

164

Believe me – I would be ashamed to boast –
Blindfold I'd name, by taste alone,
The colours of marbles, and tell most
Varieties of semi-precious stone.

LADY WALDEGRAVE:
  Do tell us, Dr Buckland, is it true,
  What has been said of you,
  That you have had a mind to feast –
  Not out of greed, I'm quite convinced –
  On every sort of bird and beast,
  On roasted mice and buzzards minced?

DR BUCKLAND:
  Quite true, quite true – not out of gluttony,
  But in a spirit of enquiry.
  The buzzard, I may say, tastes muttony,
  The texture of its flesh is wiry:
  I feel quite sure you've never heard
  It vaunted as a table-bird.
  I think that I may say
  Without the least exaggeration
  That I have eaten my way
  Through more than half the animal creation.

LADY WALDEGRAVE:
  What to your palate was the least acceptable?
  What was the farthest from delectable?

DR BUCKLAND:
  I think that on the whole,
  Dear Lady Waldegrave, quite the worst
  And nastiest was the *mole*:
  No, viler still – I once made bold to try
  What tasted quite accurst,
  A large *bluebottle fly*.

165

3. *After Dinner*

LADY WALDEGRAVE:
> We've something curious here
> For you to identify,
> We shan't give you a clue –
> Now, Mr Dean, do try!

DR BUCKLAND:
> It's very light in weight,
> Like pumice-stone, dark grey,
> I'll touch it with my tongue ...
> Volcanic, I should say.

> *Touching it with his tongue,*
> *he accidentally swallows it.*

LADY WALDEGRAVE:
> Don't say you've swallowed it! Oh, *no*!

DR BUCKLAND:
> Quite inadvertently. I felt it go
> Down like a meteorite. I feel it *here*.
> A stoppage may ensue, I fear.
> Animal and vegetable
> Are edible and assimilable,
> But such a solid lump of mineral
> Must be incomestible,
> And by this miserable sinner'll
> Prove surely wholly indigestible.

LADY WALDEGRAVE:
> Oh, Mr Dean, I understand your panic,
> But pray be calmer, I can lull it:
> What has vanished down your gullet
> Is not a stone, it is *organic*.

DR BUCKLAND:
> I feel relieved. Don't tell me! Let me guess ...
> It had a certain dryness, huskiness;

166

It was compact, and free from hair,
Like the round stone that's found inside
An avocado pear,
But dried.

LADY WALDEGRAVE:
You cannot guess, so let me speak.
It was unique.

DR BUCKLAND:
Then precious too! Forgive me! Do you think
I might imbibe some strong emetic drink
And so bring back this treasure to the light?
It did seem like a meteorite.

LADY WALDEGRAVE:
Not that! It's gone! Upon my soul
How strange the ways of chance!
That thing was bought in France.
After the Revolution someone stole
Relics from tombs. Oh, Mr Dean,
What an unheard of fate is yours!
Quite by mistake you've swallowed whole
The heart of a King! of *LOUIS QUATORZE*!

DR BUCKLAND:
I little thought I'd live to see the day
When I'd incorporate *Le Roi Soleil* –
Or even part of him.
What would he say
If he but knew an *étranger*
Had swallowed, like a pill, the very heart of him?
I fear he'd wish me harm,
I fear he'd say
'*Sale cardiophage! Quel monstre infame!*
Who gave him leave to *avaler*
Part of Our Person? *Comment? Quoi?*
Off with his *tête*! *Lèse-majesté!*
Le cœur, c'est moi!'

167

Dear Lady Waldegrave, I must take my leave.
Delightful evening! Thank you such a lot.
I've talked too much, I do believe.
Yes, I must go, my head feels rather hot.

The elixir of the grape – good gracious! –
Can, in this vale of tears, console us,
But makes an old man too loquacious:
And swallowing that unwonted bolus
Makes the room swim before my eyes.
Most humbly I apologize
For putting that royal relic out of sight.
I feel unwell ... Thank you again. Good-night.

4. *Epilogue*

LADY WALDEGRAVE:
That night Dean Buckland died. Don't laugh!
He is buried at Islip. Someone wrote
In fun, of course, an epitaph,
And this was it – you mustn't quote!

> *Here lies a Very Reverend shade,*
> *A man of parts,*
> *Who holds, till the Last Trump be played,*
> *An Ace of Hearts.*

A RIGHT-OF-WAY: 1865

[An old bass-viol was lately bought for a few shillings at a farm sale not a thousand miles from Mellstock. Pasted on the inside of it was the following poem in a well-known handwriting. It is regretted that technical difficulties prevent its reproduction in facsimile.]

Decades behind me
When courting took more time,
In Tuphampton ewe-leaze I mind me
Two trudging aforetime:
A botanist he, in quest of a sought-after fleabane,
Wheedling his leman with 'Do you love *me*, Jane?'

Yestreen with bowed back
(To hike now is irksome),
Hydroptic and sagging the cloud-wrack,
I spied in the murk some
Wayfarer myopic Linnaeus-wise quizzing the quitches
And snooping at simples and worts in the ditches.

Remarked he, 'A path here
I seek to discover,
A right-of-way bang through this garth here,
Where elsewhiles a lover
I prinked with a pocket herbarium, necked I and cuddled:
Now I'm all mud-besprent, bored and be-puddled.

'I'm long past my noon-time.
The Unweeting Planner
Again proffers bale for one's boon-time
By tossing a spanner
Or crowbar into the works without recking the cost, sir.
At eighty,' intoned he, 'life is a frost, sir.

'When erst here I tarried
I knew not my steady
Had coolly, concurrently married
Three husbands already,

Nor learnt I till later, what's more, that all three were brothers,
Though sprang they, it seems, of disparate mothers.

> 'Well, we two inspected
>   The flora of Wessex;
> More specimens had we collected
>   Had she pondered less sex;
> We botanized little that year ... But I must be wending;
> My analyst hints at amnesia impending.'

SEVEN RAINY MONTHS

March

Flip, clack! The windscreen wipers clear
A fan of focus as I take the track
To one I love, uncertain if I hear
Them or my heart repeat *Flip, clack!*

April

Like a letter-writing schoolgirl's
Over-eager punctuation
Slantwise on the window April
Dashes marks of exclamation.

May

Dulcet the half-expected shock, to hear
The cuckoo practising its name again,
Then still self-centred but not quite so near
Mocking its echo in the soft May rain.

170

June

Pattering showers on leaves undoing
Knots of guilt and anxiety freshen
The listening soul, as if the raindrops'
Muttering were a delayed confession.

July

Tidal the hush of rain all day,
Faint as the sea that haunts a shell:
Sunset X-rays a stout late bee
Nuzzling inside a foxglove bell.

August

Little more than a mist, and soon it stops:
Morning will bring that ever-pleasing sight –
Nasturtium leaves that balance trembling drops
Of quicksilver collected in the night.

September

Seed-pearl drizzle at midnight sifting softly
Out of a wide white luminous windless sky
The light of a maximum moon diffused through gauzes
Blind as the gaze of a white blind eye.

To Edith Sitwell

PALMYRA

1

Both young and forward-looking,
Much envied, you were wed:
Luck, Myra, to be hooking
That husband, gossip said.

Dream-cottage with a garage,
Brand-new, jerry-built, how trim!
How like this cosy marriage
Just made for you and him!

Watch out! There's a danger
One day if you're not wise
You'll see a sudden stranger
Stare from your husband's eyes:

Don't let him feel you wholly
Own him; if you fence him in
That enemy will slowly
Fill his familiar skin.

2

'My Pal,' she archly called him,
Or even 'Honey Boy':
Such fawning fondness galled him,
Big, grape-like eyes can cloy.

She advertised too loudly
Her new, adhesive state;
Too bold the name she proudly
Had fixed upon the gate:

172

Outside their tidy, tiny,
Too cheek-by-jowlish lair
'PALMYRA' said the shiny
New name-plate fastened there.

Oh, rashness! Who supposes
Spliced names guarantee
Well-sprung beds of roses?
Not you – and certainly not me.

3

So busy! As they found it
She thought the garden dim,
No privet hedge around it,
No workshop there for him.

Too sane the crazy paving,
She wanted it relaid,
More, and much more raving:
She ordered it, he paid.

'Cut down that tree!' she pleaded,
'Who *could* have let it stand?
Great thing! That space is needed –
Just where my rockery's planned!'

Old growth, like grace and polish,
Excites the ignoble hand
With cravings to demolish,
Drag down, or foul what's grand;

What's full, free and flowing
May madden the unfree;
New power sets them going –
Down came that noble tree:

Down crashed the shivering, twinkling
Cool poplar, which had shed
Shade, with a soothing sprinkling
Rain-sound for ears now dead.

You, Myra, saw its ending,
You withered every leaf:
How just if so offending
Makes your sojourn here brief!

4

Slugs perforate the cabbage,
Sly rust erodes the gate:
Dream-cottage with a mortgage,
Love-nest softly lined with hate:

Rows, sulks, ill-temper led to
Self-pity; Myra heard
Home-truths – but what she said to
Him gave her the last word.

He went. The door-bang shook the
Last rambler petals down:
Fed up, her Pal took the
Fast road to his home town.

No car inside the garage –
Void, like the made-up name:
That marriage was a mirage,
False fuel fed their flame;

Now only of the set-to
They had the name goes on:
Wherever does it get to,
Wedlock, when the lock is gone?

174

5

Steel windows fastened tightly
Shut out those pushing south-west
Gales, but one thing nightly
Can have, *never*, entry, rest.

Look, look! two spark-like
Moth-eyes are nudging bare
Cold glass, gleam in the dark like
Two headlights of despair.

No sound is made by bleeding,
Some nights are deathly still ...
Scratch, scratch, scratch, the pleading
Inaudible nails slip from the sill;

Palpation of small finger-tips
Not felt, feel wood and stone;
Budlike, twin and thirsty lips
Unquenchable, protrude alone;

Palmyra has this haunting,
Too much for some to bear;
Cold sceptics find it daunting,
Feel unsequestered here:

What ghost is it? they enquire.
How can they ever know?
Of unfulfilled desire
One unengendered embryo.

Man-child that Myra never bore
Pleads entry to this larger womb,
This house. For him no door
Into this longed-for living-room:

Shut out, his aim is aimless;
Unformed and lost, *lost*,
He must for ever, nameless,
Weep dew, burn white with frost.

A YOUNG JACKDAW

To have seen the poignant blue
    Of a young jackdaw's eye
Tenderer than tenderness, deeper than
    The vapour-patterned sky;
To have lent a shoulder as perch
    For this learner of earth and air,
And, featherless casual giant,
    Upheld its lightness there;

In the summer glow to have moved
    From the lime trees' emerald screen
With this trusting protégé
    Upheld, by chance, between
Worry and doubt, on a day
    When the future was running to waste –
On a day of that sort, what a drop
    Of rare wild honey to taste!

BALLADS ABROAD

SOUNDS OF PLEASURE: CANNES, 1938

The Mediterranean sighs
    Because it is so calm:
On an evening such as this
    The rustling of a palm
Seems almost ominous,
    Whispering of nemesis.

Frenchmen there are who warn
    Divided France
Of doom to come –
    Come now, it's time to dance,
The hives are full of drones,
    Hotels begin to hum.

The hissing of a crowded lift
    Going down,
The clashing open of the gate,
    The frou-frou of a gown,
High heels in a light tattoo
    Tapping to keep a date.

From the tilted bottle
    Comes the gay
Chuckle of the happiest drink;
    Cast care away!
In the glass the bubbles seethe;
    Lifted glasses clink.

Clack like castanets
    The excited dentures
Of the holder of a packet
    Of twelve per cent debentures:
For another year or two
    He can stand the racket.

Powdered arms and tinted nails
      Functioning like cranes
Sweep a wise man off his feet –
      Tonight a Princess entertains
The great Sir Mucous Membrane,
      Doyen of Harley Street.

Two exiled Kings,
      Fellow impotentates,
Dine with a diseuse
      Who cachinnates:
Oh, had their wits been half
      As quick as hers!

Loudly the rich obscure
      Applaud the Cuban band,
A rumba oils the knees
      Of the would-be grand,
And in a narrow space
      They shuffle and squeeze.

Count Lausig, who would sell
      His granny if he could,
Dances with Violet Ray
      Over from Hollywood,
And there is Susan Trout,
      Sixty, if she's a day.

The rich, how rich they smell!
      Their jewels glint like stars,
Splendid like plunder,
      Fragrant like cigars,
Like gods and goddesses they love –
      Do they? I wonder.

The sibilance of dancing feet
      Where dancing is in fashion,
The labial of a kiss,

The gutturals of passion:
Worldlings, remember all these sounds,
    There'll be an end to this.

The Mediterranean sighs
    Because it is so calm:
On an evening such as this
    The rustling of a palm
Seems almost ominous,
    Whispering of nemesis.

THE SELF-MADE BLONDE

1

The self-made blonde
    A woman of affairs
Was sitting alone
    In a room upstairs

Waiting alone
    According to plan
For the weekly visit
    Of her steady man

For her sturdy Fred
    The fitter's mate
Who never failed
    To keep the date

Wiry black hair
    And dead-white skin
His big broad bones
    And his wicked grin
For these she craved
    Like a cat grown thin

2

Fresh from the bath
    With her powdered snout
Her small brown eyes
    And her painted pout

Behind each ear
    A dab of scent
Too chastely named
    'Lilies in Lent'

She sat like a bride
    That Tuesday night
Playing patience
    By a shaded light

By a rose-pink shade
    Her bleached gold head
Was bent intent
    As the minutes sped
And her heart went thump
    For her fatal Fred

3

She plays the queen
    A move that fails
So she cheats at patience
    With her long red nails

With her long red nails
    She diddles herself
Glances at the clock
    On the mantelshelf

She pats her hair
    As bleached as tow
The king on the queen
    Alas won't go

182

The game goes badly
    She is ill at ease
The ace of spades
    Has fallen on her knees
Fred is late
    Has she failed to please?

4

She ran to the glass
    To look for a flaw
But a yearning beauty
    Was what she saw

She ran to the window
    But all was dark
Only one star
    Like an icy spark

Hope was running through
    Her heart like sand
'Oh let him stop the flow
    With his strong white hand

'I am only young once
    Let him break every bone
I will ask him to kill me
    I cannot live alone
I cannot live without him
    Or a telephone.'

5

Cut off since birth
    From the telephone
The self-made blonde
    Is as deaf as a stone

183

And mute as a doll
      Or she well might scream
To know that a curtain
      Has fallen on her dream

Insulated
      From electric Fred
Her hands grow cold
      And she feels half dead

She feels half dead
      With a nameless fear
She cannot speak
      And she cannot hear
But she goes to the cupboard
      For a bottle of beer

6

She puts two glasses
      On a fumed-oak tray
But that was the night
      The dam gave way

She picks up the bottle
      But feels no thirst
Tuesday was the night
      The dam-wall burst

A one-pint bottle
      In crimson talons
Inaudible roar
      Of a billion gallons

How can she know
      That the flood is rising
Cows are swimming
      Cars capsizing
Or find a light ale
      Appetizing?

184

7

The waters thunder
    At her own front-door
Wrench it asunder
    And submerge the floor

But up above in silence
    The self-made blonde
Endures the tortures
    Of the over-fond

Breaking up her home
    Comes the muscular flood
Carpets the carpets
    With a carpet of mud

Lifts off their feet
    The straight-backed chairs
Takes the barometer
    Unawares
And rises darkly
    Fondling the stairs

8

Against the walls
    Jostles an assortment
Of objects that have lost
    Their usual deportment

Like unread symbols
    A gate a ladder
A wireless set
    And a football bladder

Are churned around
    With an overcoat
A branch of lilac
    A bottomless boat

And the corpse of a man
      By the lamp's last beam
As it floated in
      She saw it gleam
And gave her first
      Last only scream

THE NAIAD OF OSTEND:
or, A FATAL PASSION

[In vol. I, chap. xiv, of *What I Remember* (1887), by Thomas Adolphus Trollope,
the brother of the novelist, there is an account of life at Ostend during the
bathing season of 1835. He records some of the gossip and scandals and mentions
some of the more conspicuous characters – Captain Smithett, for example, who
commanded a Channel boat called the *Arrow*, was dashing, handsome and an
immense favourite with the smart set at Ostend. Smithett showed him one day
an anonymous billet-doux which he had received, together with a latchkey.
The letter had been written by the very pretty wife of a Belgian banker, and
began: '*O toi, qui commandes la Flèche, tù peux aussi commander les cœurs.*'
    The season, says Trollope, was a very amusing one, and he had found himself
in what he calls 'a queer and not very edifying society, exceedingly strange, and
somewhat bewildering to a young man fresh from Oxford who was making
his first acquaintance with Continental ways and manners. All the married couples
seemed to be continually dancing the figure of chassée-croisez.'
    Into this evidently lively little world there came a mother and daughter, and
this is how Trollope describes them: 'We made acquaintance at Paris with a
Mrs Mackintosh and her daughter, very charming Scotch people. Mrs Mackintosh
was a widow, and Margaret was her only child. She was an extremely handsome
girl, nineteen years of age, and as magnificent a specimen of young womanhood
as can be conceived. "More than common tall", she showed in her whole person
the development of a Juno, enhanced by the vigour, elasticity and blooming health
of a Diana. She and her mother came to Ostend for the bathing season.
Margaret was a great swimmer; and her delight was to pass nearly the whole of
these hot July days in the water. Twice, or even thrice, every day she would re-
turn to her favourite element. And soon she began to complain of lassitude, and
to lose her appetite and the splendour of her complexion. Oh! it was the heat,
which really only the constant stimulus of her bathe and swim could render
tolerable. She was warned that excess in bathing, especially in salt water, may
sometimes be as dangerous as any other excess, but the young naiad, who had
never in her life needed to pay heed to any medical word or warning, would not
believe, or would not heed. And before the September was over we followed poor
Margaret Mackintosh to the little Ostend cemetery, killed by over-bathing as
if she had held her head under water! This sad tragedy brought to a gloomy end
a season which had been, if not a very profitable, a very amusing one.'
    It is on this passage that the following ballad is based.]

186

1. *The Arrival*

Ostend, eighteen thirty-five –
    Don't you know the reason
For the crowds along the front?
    It's the bathing season!

Kursaal windows flashing bright,
    Bands and fountains busy,
Pigeon-shooting, valsing, loo –
    Enough to turn you dizzy.

Such a press of elegance,
    Fribbles, belles and smarties,
Feathered heads and painted fans,
    Balls and picnic parties.

Such a flash of carriage-wheels,
    Seas of light to swim in,
Sparkling water, sparkling wine,
    Sparkling eyes of women.

Nightly, nightly now the moon
    Lights the dreaming ocean,
And at noon towards it flows
    The muslin tide of fashion.

Into this amusing world
    By the dancing-water
Enter Mrs Mackintosh
    And Margaret, her daughter.

Fresh from Paris, full of charm,
    The widow sports a bonnet
Envied for the tartans bows
    And ears of corn upon it.

187

Margaret is just nineteen,
    Tall as any goddess –
Dian in that springy step,
    Juno in that bodice.

Belgians marvel at her bloom,
    Flâneurs at her figure –
Highland mists for rosy cheeks,
    Breakfast oats for vigour.

'Mother, mother, may I bathe?'
    'Yes, my darling daughter!
See the gaily striped machines
    Drawn up to the water.'

'Mother, mother, may I bathe?'
    '*Again*, my darling daughter?'
'Ostend is so very hot,
    It's heaven in the water.'

'Mother, mother, may I bathe?'
    'Meg, my darling daughter,
I can't think where you get it from,
    This passion for the water.'

2. *The Comment*

'Your daughter seems to adore
    Above all things the sea –
She *shuns* the land, Madame.'
    'Monsieur, you're telling me!

'Three times a day she bathes,
    She finds Ostend so hot.'
'Madame, a dip is good;
    Excess, I fear, is not.'

188

'Indeed, I sometimes fear
    Some secret strange allure,
And yet I know the sea
    Is above all things pure;

'The sea's her element,
    She loves to feel aloof.'
'Ah, but a Mackintosh
    Should be more waterproof.'

3. *Social Evenings*

Fashionables delight in
    Evenings at the Fauches',
Pleasant English visitors
    Attentive on the couches;

Madame B., in yellow silk,
    Fingering the spinet,
Mary Fauche, the Consul's wife,
    Singing like a linnet.

Here and there an *œillade*,
    A look of *carpe diem* –
'Taste these sweets, they're tempting,
    Just to please me, try 'em!'

Ripe and burning August moon
    Over midnight ocean –
Neptune's manly bosom heaves
    With a deep emotion.

'Mother, mother, may I swim?'
    'What, *at night*, my daughter?
The bathing-women have gone home,
    There's *no one* in the water!'

Now the nights are dry and warm,
    And the moon grows bigger,
All the married couples dance
    The chassée-croisez figure.

Madame L., the banker's wife,
    Writes to Captain Smithett,
Sending him a billet-doux
    And a latchkey with it –

'*Toi qui commandes la Flèche*
    Peux commander les cœurs –'
History will not relate
    How he answers her.

Colonel Dickson likes to give
    Dinner parties often;
When he looks at Margaret
    His martial features soften.

Baron Melfort makes himself
    Sweet as sugar candy,
But she never turns a glance
    On that randy dandy.

Margaret turns her head away,
    Feeling bored and pestered,
Turns her lovely sea-green eyes
    Outward, seaward, westward.

4. *The Reproach*

'Margaret, I wish to find
    A husband for my daughter,
But ever since we came you seem
    Quite wedded to the water.

'The Baron with his quizzing-glass
    And wealthy Colonel Dickson
Must think you not a naiad but
    Some kind of water-vixen;

'Each is looking for a wife,
    But neither man has got a
Wish to join his fortunes with
    A two-legged female otter.

'Come out, my girl, and dry yourself,
    And let them see your figure,
Come out before your skin gets burnt
    As black as any nigger!'

'Mother, mother, I must bathe!
    Your own unruly daughter
Has found the truest, truest bliss
    Awaits her in the water.'

5. *Ecstasy*

Neptune loves the breast-stroke
    As Margaret loves the sea,
And now it is his best joke
    To keep her from her tea;

While mother bakes in dudgeon
    Beneath the hot sea-wall,
And sees her do the trudgen,
    And sees her do the crawl,

Neptune smoothes each contour,
    Each long elastic leg,
With not a soul *à l'entour*
    Embraces blooming Meg;

As supple as a porpoise
    She welcomes his advances –
Ah, Neptune, *habeas corpus*!
    The gods have all the chances.

6. *The Decline*

August grows older,
    Thunder in the air,
The pace grows slower
    In this gay Ostend,
And tarnished summer
    Seems to declare
That light abandon
    Meets a heavy end.

Parasols are folded,
    Awnings fade,
Fans still flutter
    In the afternoon shade,
They're eating ices
    In the Royal Arcade,
Soon it will be time for
    Bills to be paid.

'*Madame! et comment*
    Se porte-t-elle
Meess Marguerite?
    D'une taille si belle!'

'Thank you, she's not
    Herself, I'm afraid –
Even upon her
    This heat must tell;
She has eaten nothing
    Since Saturday night,

And seems so languid –
    It can't be right –
I'm quite alarmed –
    Uncommon pallor -
I do protest she
    Looks quite yaller.'

7. *The End*

'Mother, mother, one more bathe!'
    'Is it wise, my daughter?
I vow you owe this lassitude
    To long hours in the water.

'That is what the doctor thinks;
    Now wouldn't it be wiser
To listen to the counsel of
    Your medical adviser?

'You say the sea alone can cool
    This low and wasting fever,
But truly, truly Neptune is
    Like all men, a deceiver.'

Margaret gave her mother then
    A look that might appal,
And with a last low moan she turned
    Her face toward the wall –
    And that was all.

8. *The Epitaph*

Here lies the Naiad of Ostend
    Who swam to an untimely end,
But now with her the Cherubim
    Delight in Seas of Grace to swim;
O happy Mackintosh, to share
    That everlasting *bain de mer*!

ANGLO-SWISS:
or, A DAY AMONG THE ALPS

['Stainless steel, automatic, antimagnetic, luminous, shock-proof.'
Advertisement for a Swiss watch]

1. *The Winter Garden*

A plot of shadow by the Berg Hotel:
    Beyond that pure cobalt
Dogs in the snow look larger,
    In snow snow-white like salt;

Firs on the ridge look taller,
    The glossy jackdaws fly
Above the plateau and the salt-pan snow
    Under a stainless sky,

And up, up, up, the superlative peaks
    Hone in a howling glare
Adamant blade-like edges
    Against abrasive air:

'These are the Alps,' a brochure
    Explains, are 'peerless viewed
From the Winter Garden of the Berg Hotel
    In all their altitude'.

Snug in the winter garden
    The obvious English wait,
Rendered voracious by the rarefied air
    They sit and salivate,

Gaze at the peaks upstanding
    Of Alps they need not climb,
The Frumpspitz, the Lockstock, the Kugelhorn,
    And keep an eye on the time;

One and all they look forward
    To much and frequent food,
And eupeptic fullness seems to foster
    A self-complacent mood;

'Alpine air may be bracing
    But let me tell you this,
Swiss-made watches are antimagnetic,
    And so, I find, are the Swiss.'

That's John, an Englishman, speaking;
    He thinks he's wordly-wise
And out of his wealth of inexperience
    Presumes to generalize:

'The Swiss', he declares, 'are kindly,
    Diligent, clean, and free,
But no Swiss girl could ever wind up
    My heart's mainspring for me!

'A race of congenital waiters,
    They rightly aim to please,
But the female Swiss has about as much glamour
    As a waxwork stuffed with cheese;

'And I don't approve of neutrals –
    More cunning than the rest
Of us who have to fight for peace, they feather
    A purely selfish nest.'

'I don't agree,' said another,
    'I think you misjudge the Swiss,
You can search the world in vain for a people
    As well-behaved as this;

'Avoiding perennial bloodshed,
    Unlike the unbalanced Powers,
They've achieved a standard of decent living
    I much prefer to ours:

'How can you hold opinions
    So cheap, half-baked, untrue?
Have you ever stopped to think, I wonder,
    What the Swiss may think of you?'

2. *The Ski-Lift*

Hoisting expectant skiers
    Up from the valley below,
Up, up, up, a conveyor-belt travels
    Through snow-upholstered trees;
Bundles of raw material,
    Passively up they go
To be transformed to projectile shapes
    Launched on runaway skis;

The chair in front of him carries
    A figure John approves,
A pretty woman alone ascending
    To try the tempting slope;
As she turns her head to converse with him
    And the ski-lift smoothly moves,
Her voice and her face set moving
    The inward lift of hope:

'I hear you speak unkindly of the Swiss,'
    She says: 'Confess you do!'
(French, perhaps, from her accent?)
    'Perhaps,' he says, 'I'm wrong.'
'Oh, but have you ever stopped to consider
    What the Swiss may think of you?
How can you understand them?
    You haven't been here long!'

'I may be wrong,' he repeats it.
    'Oh yes, indeed you may,
So let me ask you to listen to a lecture
    I think it's time you heard:

196

Visting England I noticed
Only the other day
Things you forget when you try to make
The Swiss appear absurd:

'Travel on trains or buses,
You can't see out for grime,
And even when you can your urban vistas
Make little or no appeal;
Read any English paper –
A catalogue of crime!
Money is snatched by swarms of bandits
Even policemen steal;

'Rash is the girl who ventures
By unfrequented paths,
And likely to lose what is better kept
Until she is decently wed;
Children are starved and tortured,
And wives are drowned in baths,
Cupboards are crammed with strangled harlots
Dragged by the hair from bed;

'Some of your English women
Invite an end so crude –
They dress so badly, and most perversely
Cannot or will not cook;
Cigarette-smoking trollops,
Ignorant, stupid, rude,
In dirty trousers and with painted nails
How horrible they look!

'Pipe in his mouth, and so complacent
The Englishman is cold,
Far too often deserving
His narrow, graceless wife;
Dead to the fears and longings
That other hearts may hold,
His head is full of cricket and football,
Not of the art of life:

'Yours is a grasping, warlike race!
　　　I say with emphasis
Nobody loves the English –
　　　All right, I'm going to stop!
I've given a caricature of the English
　　　As you did of the Swiss –
Put it in your pipe and smoke it!
　　　But here we are – at the top!'

There at the top where skiers
　　　Confront the slopes in bliss
He can't help giving her sun-warm face
　　　A quick compulsive kiss:
'This very morning,' she teases, laughing,
　　　'You never dreamt of this!
My name is Yvette, and I must explain
　　　I happen to be Swiss!'

Away she flies and he follows,
　　　Their out-thrust profiles glow,
Already their speed is fused with the frisson
　　　That expert skiers know;
Their hearts beat fast, beat faster,
　　　Where *she* leads he will go
With a sibilant, swift and sugary hiss
　　　Over the perfect snow.

3. *The Skating-Rink*

Luminous nights in the shockproof
　　　Alps are clear and dry,
Stars don't twinkle, they stare directly
　　　Out of a sterile sky;

Metabolistic rates are quickened, the tourists
　　　Sleep-drunk bedward go,
No one is out in the village –
　　　But lights light up the snow;

198

From the Berg Hotel the ice-rink
    Looks white, looks bright, looks false –
To an empty rink an amplifier
    Repeats the Skaters' Waltz;

The Skaters' Waltz continues
    Though never a skating pair
So late competes with the flying shadows
    Flung by the arc-lamp there;

Shadows of the wind-swung arc-lamp
    Scribble across the rink
And the light at once erases those frantic brush-strokes
    Dashed on the ice like ink.

For whom are the lights all burning,
    For whom is the music played?
Silence and darkness, any Swiss can tell you,
    Can't help the tourist trade.

Suddenly a pair of skaters
    Skim into startled sight,
Obeying the invisible conductor's baton
    Under the tolling light;

Fused in a wave-like rhythm
    They sway, a gathering wave,
And a dust of diamonds fumes and sprays
    From curves their skates engrave;

One figure is it, or two there?
    One shadow, black as jet,
Waltzing distorted, expanding and shrinking,
    Commingles John and Yvette.

LUDWIG THE SECOND

['Remind me to look happier tomorrow.' *Ludwig II in a note to a servant at Hohenschwangau, April 24th, 1886*]

In this High Country of the Swan
I reign, and I am sometimes pleased
With what I plan and look upon:
So life's complexity is eased.

But not for long! Anxiety returns.
This hateful century is to blame.
Bring me some ice! My forehead burns!
Frock-coated vultures watch my name.

Bring in the lamps! I want to be alone
Yet not alone. Nobody knows how great
My loneliness and kingliness have grown.
Is it that I was born too late?

Build me a cliff-top Schloss, a ruby throne,
A resonant Wagner-Hall of Song:
I'll hear the music-myths alone.
I need a palace one mile long.

I want a million nobody will lend
To build my Chinese palace, Falkenstein.
More than pagodas I require a friend
To obey – and then command – this heart of mine.

Guilt vitiates love: they never told me that.
Each act of pleasure desecrates my dream.
Remorse runs in, quick as a rat,
A bare-tailed rat, to gnaw my self-esteem.

Gudden is not a man I care for, therefore
What is he here for? Doktor Gudden lies!
What do those other people stare for?
They're all in Bismarck's pay, all spies!

200

Order the sleigh! Send Hornig to the hut!
Is there a moon? I'm nearly ready now.
The plates are cold! See that the doors are shut!
Borrow two million! Make a lower bow!

Hold up the glass! I wish to trace
The growing sabotage of guilt and sorrow.
It is not regal, such a ravaged face:
Remind me to look happier tomorrow.

A warning oboe! Forest glades exhale
The smell of moss, a sense of loss. I'll turn and take
My downward path. Muffle the drums! I shall not fail
To fight for silence in my swan-lit lake.

BIRTHDAY BLUES

(Daisy, Princess of Pless, at Kiel, 1903)

Sun-spangled morning! Baltic June!
The yacht is clinically clean,
The summer breeze conveys from Omsk
A breath of ice and evergreen;

Paintwork all white, outside and in,
And pennants flickering like whips,
And jostling ripples keeping up
That slipshod slap against the ships;

Later of course the shadeless deck
Will burn, one's thin-soled shoes will bake –
Can I be twenty-nine to-day?
Oh, no there must be some mistake!

Though fearfully smart, this yachting suit
Did seem the fittest thing to buy –
Neat sailor blouse and short blue skirt,
White shoes, and scarlet cap and tie.

I wonder if I dress too young?
Do I? I don't know what to think;
Stout hags of forty flirt and flaunt
In frilly tulle and girlish pink;

My figure's perfect, what is *not*
Is that vile figure, 29!
A birthday if to-day must be,
Then *why* need it be *mine*?

EPIGRAMS

THE OLD CAMELLIA

Down on the clean-swept path again to-day
The old camellia drops a red rosette:
When so much grace accompanies decay
Spare us an exclamation of regret.

TWO EPIGRAMS FROM VOLTAIRE

Impromptu on Monsieur Turgot

I firmly believe in Turgot:
What he will do I don't know –
But I know it won't be, anyhow,
The same that's been done up to now.

To Monsieur Grétry

on his opera *The Judgment of Midas*, unsuccessfully played before a full house of
great lords, and very well received a few days later at a theatre in Paris.

A triumph in Paris, your songs were decried
        At court, it appears:
Alas! often the ears of the mighty
        Are mighty long ears.

THE ROAD TO HEAVEN

The road to heaven is paved with smiling faces:
Dig your heels in, and you'll see the shining places.

MY PROVERB

Lady, accept my proverb, it is yours –
A cat when pregnant should avoid swing-doors.

GIFTED DAUGHTER

'She writes because she *must*,
    My gifted daughter Ann.'
How nice! We won't pretend
    She writes because she can.

MAKING THINGS WORSE

Scratch, scratch his pen goes
    Day and night,
And much inflames his
    Itch to write.

HUNT THE HERETIC

As, once, insulting cries were heard
Of 'Dirty Protestant!' or 'Papist!'
Now, if you write of what occurred
Last week, some oaf will cry 'Escapist!'

206

OTHER POEMS

Two Abductions

EUROPA

A woman one wonderful morning
    When the dew was alive on the grass
Was washing in water like quicksilver
    And laughing at herself in the glass,

At the quivering wiry wavy
    Stiffness of her vigorous hair
Which crackled as she brushed it and shook it
    Like a burning branch in the air.

Suddenly a long dark shadow
    Came in at the wide-open door
Shutting out the rhombus of sunlight
    That lay on the tessellated floor.

She saw a stately intruder
    Pause in his swaying tread
And slowly turn towards her
    A one-idea'd head,

She saw the tremendous shoulder
    And the lustrous pearly hide
And took a last look in the glass like
    A ready and summoned bride:

Stirred by the waiting monster
    And his rolling black-and-amber eye,
The enormous promise of the morning
    And the hot florescence of the sky,

She leapt on the straight flat back
    And was carried when the tide was full
Out, far out, by the Thunderer
    To sea on a great white bull.

209

GANYMEDE

Crested and ruffed and stiff with whistling frills
Zeus as an eagle from the sky saw Troy,
Her waltzing towers and fast-impending hills,
Swerved plunging fieldwards gaitered with gold quills
To settle upon felspar and ogle the nude boy,
With plumage damascened and love-dance coy
To lure the lad, and promises of thrills.

The next day's headlines were the talk of Troy:
BIG BIRD SENSATION, MISSING LOCAL BOY.

HEADLINE HISTORY

GRAVE CHARGE IN MAYFAIR BATHROOM CASE,
ROMAN REMAINS FOR MIDDLE WEST,
GOLFING BISHOP CALLS FOR PRAYERS,
HOW MURDERED BRIDE WAS DRESSED,

BOXER INSURES HIS JOIE-DE-VIVRE,
DUCHESS DENIES THAT VAMPS ARE VAIN,
DO WOMEN MAKE GOOD WIVES?
GIANT AIRSHIP OVER SPAIN,

SOPRANO SINGS FOR FORTY HOURS,
COCKTAIL BAR ON MOORING MAST,
'NOISE, MORE NOISE!' POET'S LAST WORDS,
COMPULSORY WIRELESS BILL IS PASSED,

ALLEGED LAST TRUMP BLOWN YESTERDAY,
TRAFFIC DROWNS CALL TO QUICK AND DEAD,
CUP TIE CROWD SEES HEAVENS OPE,
'NOT END OF WORLD', SAYS WELL-KNOWN RED.

NOTE: One or two period details here may now be obscure. Vamps were coquettes, and the mooring mast was for the benefit of giant airships, for some years thought to have a future.

210

TATTOOED

On his arms he wears
Diagrams he chose,
A snake inside a skull,
A dagger in a rose,

And the muscle playing
Under the skin
Makes the rose writhe
And the skull grin.

He is one who acts his dreams
And these emblems are a clue
To the wishes in his blood
And what they make him do,

These signs are truer
Than the wearer knows:
The blade vibrates
In the vulnerable rose,

Anthers bend, and carmine curly
Petals kiss the plunging steel,
Dusty with essential gold
Close in upon the thing they feel.

Moistly once in bony sockets
Eyeballs hinted at a soul,
In the death's head now a live head
Fills a different role;

Venomous resilience sliding
In the empty cave of thought,
Call it instinct ousting reason,
Or a reptile's indoor sport.

211

The flower's pangs, the snake exploring,
The skull, the violating knife,
Are the active and the passive
Aspects of his life,

Who is at home with death
More than he guesses;
The rose will die, and a skull
Gives back no caresses.

ANGEL SATYR

['An angel satyr walks these hills.' *Kilvert's Diary*]

An angel satyr walks these hills,
But only to be seen by those
Whose fitness he divinely knows
To bear the vision and receive the seed –
The child, the virgin, and the wise,
Each in need
To be touched by his life-giving hand
And to look at his deathless eyes.

An angel satyr walks these hills
Where the child is playing alone
With a curious smooth-before-Caesar stone
Or a wind-bleached bone,
Making a fragile sap-smelling daisy-chain,
Or launching a stick-and-calico aeroplane,
Chanting a fanciful rigmarole
As he pokes a stick down a rabbit-hole,
Making a bracken lair or swinging on the branch of a tree,
Looking away up in the sky or away out to sea
For the withheld secret with unconscious expectation.

An angel satyr walks these hills
Desire become annunciation:
'All that you will be *was* before you began,
Be what you must, do what you can,
You, child, are already a man,
Hold fast to your dream. You remember the overheard
Grown-up talk, the forbidden word?
How the flower stared, the wheel went round?
How you were ridiculed when you found
Inanimate things alive? It's all true, you must know it.
Airman, your flying suit. Your slim volume, poet.
Make money, be popular, powerful, or lonely;
Be certain, doubt, cheat, or be cheated. Only
Give more than you get, and you'll get more at last.
Release what's within you. Things move fast
Only for those who are patient and free.
I give you strength to be *you*. Remember me.'

An angel satyr walks these hills,
A lurker at dusk he glows as he goes
Like a shaded lamp or a luminous rose,
And slowly, a smouldering sculpture, comes
With fixed gaze and fatal grace
To a propitious lonely place.
The virgin wandering in the lane
Suddenly meets him face to face,
Stops, cannot scream, and her heart madly drums
At the double revelation of the sacred and profane:
She is locked in a more than mortal embrace
Which unlocks the strength in her. The winter world breaks,
The unpent river, the giver, the life-building woman awakes.

An angel satyr walks these hills,
Confronts one whom the world has jaded:
'You sir, have known the worst, seen hope degraded;
You have seen the waste
Of heart, of energy, of achievement, lost your taste
For what you hungered for; so much you know,
Such muddle and misfortune around you and behind you.

213

I stand before you to show
Myself. Do I dazzle you? That is to remind you
There is always Love – in numberless forms, or seeking a shape.
I am Love in a perfect form. I show, not offer you, perfection,
That you may take heart again, escape
Sterilities of knowing, and in the veins the dull infection
Of prudence seeping. Before you I stand and shine,
Earth's essence – therefore, sir, divine.'

A CHARM AGAINST TROUBLE

The wand that speaks and the silent fruit
Have been won from the difficult tree,
And armed with these the winner can face
The evil eye that sees from afar,
The lunatic wind in the empty place,
The northern lights and the falling star,
And the gunfire thudding across the sea.

To hold that egg-like fruit in the palm,
To be even touched by that willowy shoot
Gives life, ends grief, and nullifies harm,
For the roots of the tree go down to the lake
Where we all began, where we all belong.
Turn to the world, traveller. Take
What the sap forms; the stick is in song.

214

THE SCULPTOR

In a swirl of carven vesture
On pedestal or pediment
Stone against the sky they gesture,
Embodyings all of sentiment;

Anger sometimes, battle, riot,
Leaves these history-dolls intact,
Hollow, solid, weighty, quiet,
Each accepted like a fact;

Facing all ways with their stupid
Metal foreheads, marble eyes,
Naiads, martyrs, Lenin, Cupid,
Each has much to symbolize –

Much too much! I wish to fashion
A shelter from the oppressive norm,
One step beyond the reach of passion
One crystal, non-committal form.

A TRAVELLER'S TALE

('... des horizons défaits qui se refont plus loin')

We came that way by choice,
Preferred
Desert and altitude.
That was the way we chose,
We should choose it again.

We should come that way again
Though not the men we were.
Mountain fever has left us thin,
We still see snow, the wind
That drove the grit against the skin
Has left our faces scarred,
Our cheeks have fallen in,
Our foreheads wear the anxious lines
That acid doubt takes time to groove,
But why complain?

We are not without reward
For our senses were enriched
By the difficult and rare,
The rare and strange,
The little known, the chanced upon,
Moments worth waiting for
And slowly won by weeks of care,
Moments when hope
Fell open like a shell,
And showed the pearl,
And the pearl lay in the palm.

And why did we start out?
We were impelled
To choose the way we came.
And what have we to show but scars?
Not for us to tell
Everything we know.

216

Sometimes in twos or threes,
But oftener one by one,
We made our way along
And met from time to time
Comparing notes and mapping routes.
We climbed for days towards the sky
But only came on dry plateaux
With various views
Of heights too huge to climb,
The massif, where a hooded storm
Darkens the peaks day in, day out,
But keeps the foothills green.
We cannot be too grateful
To the desert tribes,
The nomads who for shawls or beads
Helped us along,
But best of all we saw
Some pure-bred people of those parts,
Rare types, a race who act
Not for applause or momentary effect,
Who make the best of what they find
But most respect
What might exist.

All their native music comes
From instruments with just one string
Accompanied by drums,
We heard them sing
And saw them dance,
They only moved their heads and arms
But a nod of theirs means more
Than the march of crowds means here.

We heard the native names of towns
Sounding like stones let fall in pools
Or rocks rebounding between waterfalls
At daybreak into deep ravines,
But saw no towns.

Perhaps there are no towns,
Perhaps their towns
Are legends like their lives.
We know their eyes reflect
Perfections that outdo
What we conceive
At moments when the pearl
Lies perfect in the palm.

No, not the men we were
Before we came that way,
Anonymous and proud
We wear our scars with joy,
Yes, we who spent ourselves
To take a chosen way.

TASTE AND REMEMBER

To Sybil

QUEEN MARY AND THE NORWICH CROPPERS

In the hot stone of the west façade
A door was opened. Straight as a doll,
Clear as a coloured photograph,
For three seconds stood one Queen
From toque to toe illustrious
In the pale petal colour called glycine.

Her left hand light upon a shape of jade –
Contrived by Fabergé in Nineteen-Ten
To top just such a wand-thin parasol –
She saw surprising pigeons on the lawn
Crowding and hurrying on little feet
To keep up with their proud, ballooning busts.

And quickened by their oddity the Queen
In a spontaneous gesture then,
Like a young girl saluting sudden joy,
Threw up her right hand in its white kid glove.
Much too abrupt! The glove too dazzling white!
The flock took off as if they'd heard a shot.

A downward gesture then, of such regret
At having startled them to flight
In panic clatter, on their whistling wings
Circling away, away. 'Put not your trust',
Their instinct warned, 'even in princes; they
Might suddenly command a pigeon pie.'

Reticent in her pale wistaria silk
Majesty came on, planting her pointed toes,
Taking unhurriedly the plotted course
Which neither nervous birds nor ruined kings,
Great sorrow, nor a little contretemps,
Must ever, for style's or duty's sake, disturb.

SHOT AT SIGHT

Dallas! The name slaps
Its cards on the table,
Flashes a brassy brash
Probable fable
Of cold men and wild men,
Hard, bright, unstable.

Hands full of aces!
Heads full of Bourbon!
Dollars! And shark-shaped
Cars flash like platinum,
Oil kings and ranch queens
Lolling to chat in them!

To see him, well-meaning,
Willing and able,
Glide past in dry sunshine,
Precarious with power –
Young, but no safer
Than Lincoln or Gandhi!

A rifle at any man
Aimed is at all of us
Pointed, protruding
Out of a commonplace
Building, the killer
And motive both hidden.

The President passed us
With hope in his smiling:
What hope in the finger
Hooked on the trigger?
Oh, the hope that is hatred
For the better and bigger.

Now something colossal
Is seen to rise towering
From a dead politician:
Not the torch-bearing woman,
Hollow, metallic,
Who holds the false promise
Of impossible freedom,
But the image or dream
Of attainable good
All men have a hint of.
Its agents, when murdered,
Have the honour to make
That asset (our greatest)
Safe yet for a season.

READING IN THE GARDEN

Twitching upon a Mexican marigold
With lightest palpation, a pale
Chalk-blue, its tendril probe
Siphoning summer thin as a thread.

Overhead something obsessive,
A skating, shimmering nebula hangs –
Midges involved in a tribal dance:
What can one do but watch?

Reception is good for the senses today:
Too clear the chuckle, whistle,
Clatter of mad glad starlings,
Bossy and glossy, plebeian.

It is not easy in an August garden
To read with attention. Two books
Wait beside me, neither a flower
I feel drawn to sip.

223

A new book by an old man,
Sampson Tanner; long a stranger
To new ideas, he answers
His own dull questions.

Live long and keep crowing,
People can't help hearing:
Uncovetable fame, to crow
On a stale heap of self-esteem!

A young girl wrote the other:
Open lilies her five senses,
Each a mirror busy with
Her image from all angles:

Behind the mirrors a black screaming
Void full of lost voices,
Behind the buttonhole mouth
Fear straining, greed growing:

Rosy nails skipping brittly
On her nimble little portable
To add a book to all books –
What can she think she knows?

Lucinda Stoat-Smith,
Heiress of all the ages,
Why are you here
And why with me?

Well, you're here. To think
Old Tanner's here too!
Sir and madam, life is all
Metamorphoses.

Mine is a more than midway,
An afternoon moment, where
Life is not snatched or guzzled,
Nor clung to, but all in view.

A seized perspective is no heroic,
Epic subject; in a calm between
The age of war and the flight to space
Simple things loom large.

One might expect in an August garden
Besides heat and a cold drink
The semi-coma of a quiet mind,
But visibility is acute today:

Showy the grass, as if painted green;
Teasing, piggish, the odour of phloxes
All staring with crimson eyes;
Traffic nags, nags at a distance.

Slow, dazzling clouds recall
An irretrievable dream-England
Visioned once in the warm light
Of half delusion, half truth;

A land of everlasting elms
Mothered by the round white clouds,
Dream-days, anaesthetized,
Without wheels, without wounds.

Not like that now
With jet-engines overhead!
It is not easy to relax in the garden
Under a canopy of strident threats.

As for me, I sit here,
Once young, not old,
Able to think of the dead, the growing,
The unborn, on a summer's day.

If my grandfather were alive today
His age would be a hundred and forty;
And Marie, my godchild,
How old is she now?

225

Small person, she banged on the window
With both hands, in wild longing
To be out of doors with us,
Danced with rage; she was five then.

Windows, bolts, bars, bans,
Melt as the child grows tall;
She is out in the open now,
Is about to be fifteen;

Is out of doors with us all,
With us all now, all
Our folly – O may
She have my luck!

Not hungry, not penniless,
Not deaf yet, blind, or lame,
Not yet in the poor-house –
Precarious to be me, here, now!

Not yet in the pest-house,
Mad-house, dead-house,
But outside a dwelling-house
In August, in a long chair, musing.

It is not easy to be calm as if
The air we breathe were not corrupt,
Not full of the dirty floating
Corrosive filaments of hate and lies.

All the same, I am conscious of privilege,
Of being sustained by stress and effort
Over a long time, by many,
And so brought to this place,

This after-midway moment.
So, with a sense of obligation
I take up and open
A book – never mind which.

Oh, but this minimal, ephemeral
Insect speeding on the page –
What a risk! How very precarious
To be it, here, now!

Whether the book is Tanner's or Lucinda's
A turn of the page would blot it out:
Impermanence we have in common –
We have life too.

The music of a huge joy swells,
Rises, floods my veins and bones,
And the fine nerves of my skin tingle:
This is life, it feels like hope.

Man means murder, plans
Self-murder too. Apart,
Of that I still am part.
How next to act?

The clear head, the full heart,
Telling us what to do
Are not heeded, not heard:
Of all our talents, misuse.

But while a whim can change
Us all to glass and gas,
As if all's well
We swim towards the stars.

Let the wren build its nest
Next year, as it did this,
If it can, if it's here;
We live by an *As if*

I read on as if
Hoping the book has point;
We live as if
Reason could allow hope.

227

A WALK IN WÜRZBURG

Passing a dull red college block
Of the bygone, full-fed, Kaiser time,
When the tribal mercury welled up
Ready to burst, is to wonder if inside
That institute some intent and hairy head,
Bored by the strut of the show-off turkey-cock,
Through steel-rimmed ovals used at that time perhaps
To peer with love, pure love, of finding out;

Is to wonder who now may be tunnelling there
For an unknown vein, or perhaps with the sifting hand
Of an archaeologist-in-reverse
Dredging towards a treasure the future hides.
Bombs broke the wigged Baroque only yards away,
But his thoughtful back would be that of a sage
Averted from fractured dreams, unhealable wounds,
Revenges, ruined walls, undruggable nerves.

By chance to see an inconspicuous plaque
On that otherwise unadorned wall, is to learn
That here, right here, a miracle struck
Which altered us all – as Gutenberg did,
Daguerre, or Freud; is to feel what the pious feel,
Quite carried away to find they face
Unawares a place of sublime prestige,
Where a saint flared out of the chrysalid stage.

Not to have known about this! That here,
That nowhere else in the wasteful, wilful,
Death-wishing world, here Röntgen focused his ray
And the eye first saw right through the skin,
So that now without knives we see what is wrong
Or is going to be wrong. We still need a ray
To coax the delicate wings from the commonplace husk
And detect why the horde we are destroys itself.

NOTE: This poem appeared originally in the *New Yorker*; the author is grateful
for permission to reproduce it here.

THE HALF-RECLUSE

['Far better to be a half-recluse.'
Po Chü-i (A.D. *829*)
translated by Arthur Waley]

More than a thousand years!
  I thank you, first and last
  Of poets to define
  A way of life I see
    As not remote from mine.

More than a thousand years!
  I feel that I belong
  Within the self-same age
  That once gave you, and now
    Gives me half-hermitage.

More than a thousand years;
  But now a break has come.
  Would communists condemn
  Semi-reclusiveness
    And disapprove of us?

But not a thousand years
  Are needed to perceive
  That best a poet's heart
  Invents its distillates
    In pulsing half apart.

A BRIEF ABSENCE

Back on Tuesday – not, I hope,
Who Monday went away from you –
What do I bring you to make up
For taking a night and day from you?

When absence made the heart go wander –
As it used, oh yes, it used to do –
With easy come and easy go
The weeks on wheels of moonshine flew.

But now, but now, your gentleness
And fierceness, blent in one, evoke
A quite new self, a ruby fire,
A Tuesday flame to Monday's smoke.

LIME-FLOWER TEA

The esplanade empty, closed at this time
    The gates of the park;
The sea waveless, only a murmur
    In the formless dark
Of a night in winter; frost fusing
    Glass beads of drifted snow,
Trashy remnants of a white glare
    One dazzling day ago.

Frost hardens, glazes, grips; on glass
    Will damascene
Traceries tonight of ferns.
    A plain screen
Of fog has curtained off the sea.
    Street lamps illuminate
A livid emptiness, and one man,
    Only one, walking late.

230

He stops walking, stands then, vaguely gazing
  Is amazed to hear
Gentle flutings of seabirds,
  Unseen but near –
Communings of pure confidence,
  Intimations of their ease
And of a separate togetherness
  No arctic night could freeze.

Each flute-note has made him think
  Of his own life –
Quiet years with a neurotic
  Childless wife:
On a winter night, when needling frost
  In total silence etches ferns,
He to her like a seabird speaks,
  She, wingless, to him turns.

His walk alone at night she understands
  And the unsaid;
In the warm room she'll pour out,
  Before bed,
Delicately, lime-flower tea;
  Together they will sip and dream,
Sad and content, both drugged
  By the lost summer in the scented steam.

Two Portraits

MRS MIDDLEDITCH

Fitting a thin glove
Over a dry hand,
Over a gold ring (plain
As the nine-carat love
Of her good man now dead),
Mrs Middleditch pats
For the sake of tidiness
The back of her tidy head.

'It's time for shopping again.
I must think of the things I need,
Or *think* I need. Time
To go out. If I stay in
I mightn't go out at all.
I might give way to doubt
And ask, What *is* it all *for*?
And not go out of my door:

'And think, Why leave my bed
To wash and dress and eat,
And wash up, and wash out a dress,
And dress up, and go out to tea?
Sameness of fading days,
Is this what life should be?
Am I the slightest use?
And who would ever miss *me*?

'I must make out a list,
I suppose a widow must eat:
A caterpillar must eat –
But then, it can hope for wings.

Floor polish, cocoa, cake,
Sago, margarine, yeast –
A gruesome menu there
For my lonesome evening feast!'

'Oh, Mrs Middleditch, good
Morning to you!'
                    'And to you!'
'A lovely morning again!'
'It is. (But you give me a pain;
What goes on in my head
You neither care nor guess;
One can have a little too much
Bright neighbourliness.)'

At the Supermarket door
An amplifier hails
Each housewife – and her purse –
With smooth false bonhomie.
Could anything be worse?
Mrs Middleditch hears
With a shiver of distaste
These words affront her ears:

'A Supermorning, madam,
For Supermarketing!
Our cut-price Superfoods
Are best for each and all,
Our Supergoods await you
On every Supershelf,
So take a Superbasket
And help your Superself!'

'Oh, Mrs Middleditch,
This place *is* a boon!
I've come here for everything
Since my honeymoon.'

'Yes, yes, convenient,
Marvellous, I agree –
And yet I feel somehow as if
It's pressing in on me:

'There's too much of everything,
Too much advertisement,
I ask myself if what is said
Is ever what is meant –
FISH FLAKES *taste breezy*,
CAKE FIX *bakes lightest*,
QUICK WAX *makes work easy*,
SQUELCH *whitens whites whitest*.'

'Oh, Mrs Middleditch,
Excuse me if I ask it.
But you've not got a single thing
So far in your Superbasket!
Let me recommend these peaches
And the nice thick double cream,
And you'll find the chicken breasts
(Milk-fed, of course) a dream.'

'I've got a list of things I need
Or thought I needed. Now I know
That peaches, chickens, cream,
And even sago, cocoa, yeast,
Are things I cannot buy today.
Today I fast, not feast.
I can't put out my hand, I find
A double vision in my mind.

'Beyond abundance – butter, eggs,
Strength-giving meat and cubes of cheese,
And cylinders of beans and peas
And syrup-swimming halves of pears –
Deserts I see, and frowsty rags,
And groups of persons wearing these,
Bowed by the weight of nothingness;
I recognize them – refugees.

234

'I see a child with seething flies
Fouling its big, unblinking eyes,
Eyes fixed on me: a swollen child
With dangling, thin, rachitic wrists,
Listless and silent, watching me,
In want and in unwantedness
Waiting to learn why it was born –
While I draw up my shopping lists.

'It will not do! I have no appetite
For food. And none for charity!
Dull, shiftless outcasts under static skies,
They are myself. Only the pelican
That tore her breast could teach me how
To reach that place, to staunch with work
That open sore, to feed with love
One orphan fed upon by flies.'

'Oh Mrs Middleditch! Are you all right?'
Her answer was a sudden moan
And down she slumped upon the Superfloor,
The spotless floor of Non-Slip Superstone.
Inside her Superbasket was her head,
Unconscious prisoner of a Supercage.
'Quick, call the manager!' 'She was acting strange.'
'Silly old fool! she's reached the awkward age.'

(1960)

THE MONEY MAN

I got in. I didn't expect
Notice, and got none from the white
Miser in black, opposite, sifting
News from the City, reading that day
How *Oils were inclined to ease*
(Surely that is what oils are for?)
And *Rubber continued dull.*

To him it may have seemed news;
Never an outgoing man
He seemed, without heat or light
And quite disinclined to ease.
But how could one judge without knowing?
To Balzac he might have appeared
Though money-obsessed, a saint.

At Kingham got in a youngish
Woman, *en beauté*, a rose
In the shadow of roses, at ease
In some man's love and a new
Fur coat. She made the morning
Shine, her obvious happiness made
The journey quite first-class.

You'd think he might have looked up,
Not warmly appraising but mildly
Inquiring, then she would accept
(Not take for granted, being quite
Unassuming) the slight homage
Of hopeful maleness, catching a glint
Of at least not being ignored.

From me she received – to show I agreed
One's best is not for oneself –
An open look: but the money man
(The skin near his mouth the dead

Skin of a dried haddock) had turned
His monomaniac eyes
On perhaps more rewarding news:

Perhaps content he had sold his shares
In THROGNEEDLE LOANS, relieved
He had kept, in view of a rising trend,
His OFFAL-PROCESSING TRUST,
And glad to learn he was soon to receive
An interim dividend
From CHEERIO INSTANT WINES ...

Paddington ran to meet us. Steely
Rails brought eternity racing
To lassoo us three
And profit and loss. He turned his head.
From one ear dangled what seemed
A strand of spaghetti – his hearing aid.
He looked at us. He smiled. He spoke:

'This train, besides being dirty, is late.
One doesn't know to whom to complain,
Or who would listen. And I can't hear.
And if I could, I shouldn't believe
A word. To me life seems
A confidence trick: my wife has been
For years insane. Good day.'

Show Business

A SUMMER STORM

This is the voluntary patients' wing,
This is the lounge, and that old dear
Watching the storm is eighty-nine.
She was an actress once: she is one still.

Flash, flash! The lightning snapshots eagerly
Her simpering bloodless face. With drums,
Big drums, thunder explodes and roars
And shakes the world and us: it can't shake her.

'So many flashlight photographs,' she beams,
'The whole press must be here. Oh, what a house!
They want a speech. Oh thank you, thank you all!
You're all so kind, you will be glad to know

'My doctor says my arteries are like
A woman of fifty's. Yes, he thinks I'm wonderful,
I know you'll all be glad to know he says
That if I'm careful I'll outlive myself.'

And as the velvet curtain of the rain
Slowly descends, the obsolete crinkled face
Displaces all its map of criss-cross paths
And forms what is intended as a smile,

And the force of habit lifts a colourless claw,
An old hen's foot, to blow a kiss.
God help us all, is this what habit does?
Let us not act as *us*, and end like this.

NOT WHERE WE CAME IN

'This is not where we came in,
The story has all gone wrong.
Don't you remember, we saw
Terraces, vistas, marble urns,
Magnolias of human skin, a tall
Carved door, and that low superb
Smooth car? Between the two
The perfect girl was poised, to lead
With the scent of her physical pride
A millionaire playboy wolf
And a polished, lecherous duke.
It was what we had paid to see –
An epic of processed tripe.

'But the story has all gone wrong,
Her castle was pastry, her diamonds dew,
Her glossy hair is withered,
Her shoe-heels are abraded.
Just look at the girl, would you know her?
A refugee drab, she's lugging
A suitcase full of grudges
That nobody wants to buy.
Look at her now, she's pointing
Straight at us. She's armed. She's speaking.
"It's *you*, and *you*, and *you*
To blame. Take *that*! and *that*! and *that*!"
My God, she's real! I'm shot! It's blood!'

BEFORE THE CRASH

Caught sight of from the car
(Just before the crash)
On the river bank
    Against a hanging cliff of bronze
    A great white colony
    Of resting and of nesting swans.

In marble attitudes
(Distant, as things are
Living their own lives)
    The swans, arranged in twos and threes,
    Were doing nothing; we
    Were doing eighty – and with ease.

Seen also from the car,
Minutes and miles along,
Flames in a ballet stretch
    Enormous up from straw and trash
    In frenzy to attain
    The coda – just a little ash.

Tempi of swans and fires,
Cars, and suns beyond
Furnace-roaring suns
    No man will ever hear – in space
    These harmonize, none are
    Winners or losers in a race.

THE LAST TRAIN

Suddenly awake at two, and aware of the disintegration
Of silence by the distant but steadily growing louder
Travelling of a multitude of metal, a remnant of a regiment
Of defeated men in armour overweighted by retreat,
Without hope, late, lost, but continuing all along
In the habitual rhythm of discipline, of one last order obeyed.

That's what it is! Of course it is the last, the very last
Train; they said it would go past tonight, the long
Last train of all, before the closing of the line.
Under a clear chill moon, loud now but growing no louder
In clattering concatenation it goes reverberating on
Unhurried, and clanking already, already, a little less loud.

They make it give out a long clear whistle, a thrilling
Scream as of some rare owl when huge-eyed at knowing
Itself last of all its kind its utterance is despair;
It is a brontosaurus lumbering off into the ultimate
Exile of solitude, without mate or progeny, unadaptable,
Wielding in a laborious gait its huge unwanted limbs.

Extinction is signalled. This is the end of the Age of Steam
(Like all others a devouring age) and with it one more
Realized fantasy of power has receded into history;
The ancestral pistons seem like playthings now, the linked-up
Old iron trucks and bogied cars of this last trundling train
And their knocking rhythm dwindling along the impermanent
    way.

They carry a weightless load of dissolving associations –
A scented fug on an autumn day in the Orient Express;
And the persevering Trans-Siberian scattering scarlet sparks
Into the eyeless Mongol dark; and the locomotive bell
Clanging its lonely threat as someone took the prairie way
To the punishment of banishment, along the Atchison-Topeka
    line to Santa Fé.

241

EXIT LINES

Sun laid a cinnabar tint
On his wife's white arm
As she poured in his cup
Coffee, a black glass rod.

Faintly uneasy to see
His name in an unknown hand,
He opened a letter, and read:

'If you knew that on Monday week
You were to die in your bed,
And if you were asked
For a sentence or two
To be remembered by,
What would you say?

'I don't mean a planned attempt
At would-be famous last words,
Or a thought-out parting shot –
And no heroics, please –
But that those who hear you speak
(If there is time to speak
And if you can shape your thought)
May remember whatever you say.

'In fact on Monday week
You'll reach the end of your life.
This isn't a threat or a hoax,
The unexpected cause
Of your death is natural.
My precognition I give,
But prefer to conceal my name.'

And so to Monday week.
Silent his wife and summoned kin;
Deathbedside-mannered, the nurse;
And a friend all ready to note
The exit lines.

'Weaker now,' said the dying man.
'There is something I want to say.
If ever you have to choose
Either to stick to a way of life
That goes against your plans,
Habits, ambitions, beliefs,
Or, by quitting it, kill
Or wound that wild animal, love –
Well, you know what is best to do.
Wild animals cannot speak;
They watch with their constant eyes.'

He had only the time to say
With his last, overdrawn strength
In a low but audible voice,
'You may ask what I mean by love?
I suggest you give the word all
The weight you think it will bear.'

And after a moment he said,
'When your own breath has blown
A clear, symmetrical vase,
Don't you be the one to break
The flesh-coloured glass.'

His wife
Covered her face with her hands.

Two Elegies

THE SHORTEST DAY

Fume of fine food and room-warmed wine
In a warm high room above the sea;
Hint of narcissus in the air displaced
By a woman moving; two men with cigars;
Windows wide open on a frosted, waiting day –
The shortest day. Aroma of living, savour of being,
Of well-being, chemistry of sympathy, accord,
Life at a height, warm life – and yet
         All is not well.

Today there is no horizon, the increasing towns
Are all one town, stopped only by the shore.
Along the edge of the water's vast taboo
Cars pause, that have bred like flies, and buzz
On the puzzling glass of winter, by that cut off
From the white, quiet, boatless, motorless,
Shortest-day sea. Drifts of resentful cars
Edge out, drone off, freeing from their dull gaze
         The waveless sea.

The sea, a breathing opal, lifts and lets fall
And lifts again a cruising indolent shoal
Of coppery flakes from the smudged and smouldering sun;
Out there the stillest day; out there
The engine of the sea is idling, giving
Now and then an undulant shudder, raising
A wavering edge; then the desolate sigh and hiss
Of the merest wavelet, an accent on silence
         Filling the room.

Up there just then no talk of the past, of its
Folly and mania, impulses, appetites, accidents;

244

Frenzies of adolescence; journeys in vain;
Anxiety throbbing like a disease;
The axe of bereavement; the bait of hope
On the hook of failure; electric delights;
Trust growing slowly. Physical beauty still
Imbues and graces all three. It cannot make
            Plain joys hold fast.

Out there horizontal calm; yes, but a
Stage for horrors performed – only the sea's
Are not acted, are real; they continue.
Each in that room, on a different stage
Or ocean voyage, was geared by a compromise,
The woman a sail that carried a man along,
One man by devotion powered and steered,
The other set on a predetermined course
            Of no return.

Each was involved in rhythms not one
Had foreseen or intended. The woman could ever
Taste again the dreamy mutuality known
To the young. The watchful man had a lasting
Love that was duty, whole-time. The other
Was already a long way off, and spoke
To the others over a chasm. (The courage of somewhat
Privileged persons may merit more praise
            Than it may get.)

The shortest day is soon over. Afternoon
Hardly occurs. Day's pearl dulls. The not much
Uprisen sun has gone blurred and glimmering by.
From that high room soon to disperse,
Now from the window they watch from its frost-cocoon
The sun float free – bare, huge and red.
'Just look at the sun!' 'But who can tell
What it possibly means? Does it mean STOP
            Or DANGER – which?'

245

Later a little, livid, the lulled sea slid
One way, from east to west, a satin dyed
With ebbing light, endlessly drawn along
From day's vat into the dark. Great liquid lake,
It is a distillation of the drowned. Even just then
Perhaps, not far away, and quite unseen
Was entering into it, too intent to feel
Its venomous ache, some loneliest, dowdiest suicide
          Waist-deep, alone.

The woman is not in the room, has left like a scarf
Her trail of narcissus. The man has gone, for whom
In marriage is order. That other looks out, alone,
And the calm is for him a terrible pause.
For some there is no sedation, not in a high warm room
Above the December sea; in company, they are apart,
And homeless at home; and love, of which they hear much,
Is a distant light. Facing the sea now, he
          Dreams of the drowned.

Of that suicide, received in a total embrace
By water, to be translated into the basic
Language of being, reassumed into the unending
Dance of the elements, the chain of reviving,
Dissolving shapes, needs, impulses. In that
How can he possibly find what some may suppose
Exists, and presume to call a 'meaning'?
Who on earth can read a language
          Quite beyond words?

If men are made in the image of God, then
No two being alike, each is a different glint
Of a diamond much flawed, or a cheque drawn
On an inexhaustible account, a syllable
In a story still being written. Unending millions
Of try-outs are tried out as if for a purpose
And then discarded, dissolved, rejected;
Millions of differing, vanishing images are what
          God makes man in.

How many have vanished at sea! A slave ship at noon
Unchains only the sick; prone with fever and despair,
Ebony giants lose value; robed only in their last sweat,
Still breathing, still seeing, are jettisoned to sharks.
Or on some calm spring night breaks out a screech
Of grinding metal, waterfalls, fire bells; in cabins tilting
Bewildered children are snatched up from sleep
By love as the ship sinks. But there is no help.
        They are not saved.

Up a vertical wave a raft swoops, against it
Three sailors are snails glued on a wall;
False hope is the force that holds them there;
They were armed; they are unarmed now; one slips,
The last two lose hold; the raft rears up,
The last one now, as the raft plunges, is gone.
What is it all for? Now against a new cliff
Of ice-green water hangs a blackboard with no lesson –
        The raft is blank.

The shortest day has sunk in the longest night,
In a coma of cold. The watcher alone up there
About to exclude the dark, must turn to face
A darkness within; but now sees one small light
Putting out to sea, with the vibrant vigilant beat
Of the motor of one small boat. To be so slight
Seems impertinent, in the knowledge that out from here
To the rocks of eternal ice, all is water
        And half is night.

Life isn't only a slave ship, a shipwreck; it's also
An outgoing boat with an outboard motor at night
Pitter-pattering off with a confident impetus
Into the dark with its light, into the frost with its heat,
Into the end of the night. The atlas avers
That the place remains, that turbulent place,
And the name, that marvellous name, persists;
Yes, even that soul up there was bound for his own
        Cape of Good Hope.

247

THE TASTE OF THE FRUIT

[In memory of the poet Ingrid Jonker, who was found dead by night
at Sea Point, Cape Town, in July, 1965; and of Nathaniel Nakasa,
the South African writer, who died by suicide in the United States in the
same month.]

Where a dry tide of sheep
Ebbs between rocks
In a miasma of dust,
Where time is wool;
He is not there.

Where towers of green water
Crash, re-shaping
White contours of sand,
Velvet to a bare foot;
She is not there.

Where pride in modesty,
Grace, neatness,
Glorify the slum shack
Of one pensive woman;
He is not there.

Where one fatherly man
Waited with absolute
Understanding, undemanding
Hands full of comfort;
She is not there.

Where sour beer and thick smoke,
Lewdness and loud
Laughter half disguise
Hope dying of wounds;
He is not there.

Where meat-fed men are idling
On a deep stoep,
Voicing disapproval
Of those who have 'views';
She is not there.

Where with hands tied
They wrestle for freedom;
Where with mouth stopped
They ripen a loud cry;
He is not there.

Where intellectuals
Bunch together to follow
Fashions that allow for
No private exceptions;
She is not there.

He, who loved learning,
Nimbly stood up to
The heavyweight truth;
For long years in training
He is not there.

She was thought childlike
But carried the iron
Seeds of knowledge and wisdom;
Where they now flower,
She is not there.

A man with no passport,
He had leave to exile
Himself from the natural
Soil of his being,
But none to return.

She, with a passport,
Turned great eyes on Europe.
What did she return to?
She found, back home, that
She was not there.

Now he is free in
A state with no frontiers,
But where men are working
To undermine frontiers,
He is not there.

'My people', in anguish
She cried, 'from me have rotted
Utterly away.' Everywhere
She felt rejected;
Now she is nowhere.

Where men waste in prison
For trying to be fruitful,
The first fruit is setting
Themselves fought for;
He will not taste it.

Her blood and his
Fed the slow, tormented
Tree that is destined
To bear what will be
Bough-bending plenty.

Let those who savour
Ripeness and sweetness,
Let them taste and remember
Him, her, and all others
Secreted in the juices.

CELEBRATIONS

[1]

A NOTE FROM A CELLO

[In the summer of 1969 the Maltings, the great concert-hall
near Aldeburgh, was destroyed by fire. These lines were written to
celebrate its restoration in 1970.]

A blameless calm night, the people have gone.
Dark thickets of reeds feel a breath of disquiet:
Moorhens awake; fear saves the vole
About to be hooked by the soft-flying owl;
In the marshes of Snape a sluice and a pool
Make suddenly shapes of flame-coloured light.

A crackle of fire! An undeclared war,
Motiveless, strikes at those who contrived
That resonant shell, at ears that have heard
Rejoicings derived, in nights darker by far,
From far greater fires, wells deeper, deep dreams,
Granite, violets, blood, the pureness of dew.

The shell is restored. The orchestra settles.
A baton is raised. Renew what is old!
Make known what is new! From a cello the bow
Draws its hauntingest tone, confiding, profound;
And immured in the bone the marrow responds
To the endless, exploring inventions of sound.

A CHURCH IN BAVARIA

Everything flows
   upward over
      chalk-white walls
         with the ordered freedom
            of a trellised creeper
         wreathed and scrolled
      in a densely choral
anthem of ornament.

Nimble angels
   poise above
      in attitudes,
         huge-limbed prophets
            banner-bearded,
         giant apostles,
      mitred titans
   exemplify
authority,
   their garments ribbed
      in whorls and folds,
         corrugations
            of pearly grace,
         sea-shell volutions
      turned by ages and
oceans of prayer.

Visions of Paradise
   pivot their rolling
      eyeballs upwards,
         their lips issue
            garlands of praise,
         flexible
      they bend from narrow
waists, and raise
   smooth rounded arms
      with hands adoring

or holding golden
   instruments,
      long fingers fingering
    tingling harps,
  long trumpets sounding
triumph unending.

Everything flowers
  in aspiration
    to an imagined
     culmination,
      the athlete spirit's
     endless training
   gives ecstatic
 buoyant lightness,
all aspires as
  shaped and soaring
    white and ring-dove
    grey and gilded
      formal figures
    in a sacred dance.

  What does all this
  joyful brilliance
have to do with
  cults obsessed with
    guilt and sin,
     a punishing angry
      vindictive God?
    Where's that hard
   right-angled object
the Cross, with Victim
  blanched by torture,
  dead, with blood?

    Here the focal
     point discloses
      a seated Virgin,
     her covered head

257

at a fond angle
in accord with
all this swaying
   court of images,
      looking down
         benign and gentle
            at the incredible
fact, her Child.

Everything sings
in snowy stillness,
in marble wonder,
   in formal myth,
      believed because
         impossible,
            believed as only
         a poem can be,
      the anti-fact
of a holy spore
spreading the Word
   unsaid before.

Everything bends
   to re-enact
      the poem lived,
         lived not written,
      the poem spoken
   by Christ, who never
wrote a word,
   saboteur
      of received ideas
         who rebuilt Rome
            with the words he
         never wrote;
      whether sacred,
   whether human,
himself a sunrise
   of love enlarged,
      of love, enlarged.

A CASUAL ENCOUNTER

(In memory of Cavafy, 1863–1933)

They met, as most these days do,
among streets, not under leaves; at night;
by what is called chance, some think
predestined; in a capital city, latish;
instantly understanding, without words,
without furtiveness, without guilt,
each had been, without calculation, singled out.

Wherever it was they had met,
without introduction, before drifting this way,
beneath lamps hung high, casting
cones of radiance, hazed with pale dust,
a dry pollenous mist that made
each warm surface seem suede, the sense of touch
sang like a harp; the two were alone.

To be private in public added oddness,
out of doors in a city with millions
still awake, with the heard obbligato
of traffic, that resolute drone,
islanding both, their destination
the shadow they stood in. The place
should perhaps be defined.

But need it? Cliff walls of warehouses;
no thoroughfare; at the end a hurrying
river, dragonish; steel gates locked;
emptiness. Whatever they said
was said gently, was not written down,
not recorded. Neither had need
even to know the other one's name.

Nor do you need to know any more
of an hour so far off, so far,
it may be, from what turns you on.
They, with peacefullest smiles at a rare
Befriedigung, parted, breathing the gold-
dusted, denatured air like the pure
air of some alp: nor met ever again.

Is that all? To you it may seem
a commonplace episode. Once was a man
who might not have thought so. To him
(an old photograph hides his neck clamped
in a high stiff white collar, on his pale face
a false-looking moustache) let me dedicate
this moth-winged encounter, to him, to Cavafy himself.

NOTE: I had some correspondence with Cavafy and dedicated a poem
to him. He politely said he was proud of it, but I did not think well enough
of it to reprint it in my *Collected Poems*. Possibly he might have preferred the
present offering.

   The old photograph referred to was in a voluminous anthology of modern
Greek poetry which I picked up in Athens in 1930. Many of the photographs
with which it was illustrated were of soulful and sentimental-looking poetasters.
Cavafy's face, photographed perhaps near the beginning of the century, stood out
among them by its gravity and dignity.

THE AXE IN THE ORCHARD

[In the summer of 1911, when Chekhov had been dead for seven years,
The Cherry Orchard was first performed in London. It was afterwards reported
that at the end of the second act 'signs of disapproval were very manifest indeed,
and the exodus from the theatre began'. By the end of the third act half the
audience had departed.]

Nothing was heard but a whisper
Of satin. A notable couple
   Were shown to their places,
Well mated, assured, and upholding
An air of combined high command on
   Their thoroughbred faces.

Sir Something and Lady Someone
(No one remembers them now) –
   She, an Edwardian goddess
With a helmet of maid-brushed hair,
Pearls, and two velvet roses
   Blush-pink in her bodice,

To people she knew bowing slightly,
With the soldierly head of Sir Something
   More rigidly slanted,
His important moustache manifesting
Its wearer a person deferred to,
   Not taken for granted.

Oh, why were they there at the theatre?
They were idle, not curious; a hostess
   Ought to be able,
Lady Someone believed, to show up-to-dateness
And stimulate talk about plays among
   Guests at her table.

Between them and the stage loomed a spectral
Wave-ruling flagship, obscuring
   The sense of the show;
Sir Something and Lady Someone
Never guessed it was doomed and would founder,
   The ship *Status Quo.*

Sir Something's cold glare at his programme
Was like that he turned on from the Bench
   At some rustic offender;
Nothing was heard but his 'Well, now'
(Meaning 'Let's get it over'),
   'Let's see the agenda.'

'Who is this feller? A Russian?
Never heard of him, what? But I bet
   He can't hold a candle
To Arthur Pinero. God help us,
These damn foreign names! Four acts of it, too!
   I call it a scandal.'

Lady Someone said, 'Hush, dear, I know.' She
Was used to his testy complaining.
   Soon nothing was heard
But his mutter, 'Impossible people!
Dull twaddle! Nothing is *happening*!
   The whole thing's absurd!'

Disapproval can circulate quickly;
By the end of Act Two he declared it
   High time to go,
And they rose, with their vertical backbones,
To snub this *new* playwright they'd settled
   Was worthless to know.

But, as was ordained, when the actors
Had gone, when the stage was deserted,
   At the end of the play,
Nothing was heard but the strokes of
The axe in the orchard, the strokes
   Of the axe far away.

The strokes of the axe in the orchard
Soon grew louder, unbearably thudding
   By night and by day;
Then nothing was heard but the guns in
The orchards of France. All at once Russia
   Was less far away.

THE PLANES OF BEDFORD SQUARE

Never were the plane trees loftier, leafier,
the planes of Bedford Square,
and of all that summer foliage motionless
not one leaf
had fallen yet, one afternoon
warm in the last world-peace before
the First World War.

At Number Thirty, consulate
of the very last Czar,
before a window on the tall first floor
Baron H., the consul, dreamy
with a Flor de Dindigul cigar,
saw the slow smoke
ghosting an arboreal form.

Tennis was thudding underneath the trees
on grass close-shorn.
A quick racquet flashed
the thump of a return,
and a young voice called the score
as if all was for the best
everywhere, not only on this marked-out lawn.

And all the soaring trees, a tree-of-heaven among them,
wore their enormous shawls of leaves
in full dress, over the court, over
the railed-in shade. Not one leaf,
not one, was yet to fall. On the first floor
was there yet one thought, one
forethought of compulsive and appalling war?

Firbank had started carving hardstone
tesserae to fit his semi-precious prose,
had fondly made a bishop's daughter yearn
'Oh, I could dance for ever
to the valse from *Love Fifteen*!',
foresaw perhaps that she might burn
to ash without one invitation to a ball.

In this well-ordered square the front door yawned
of Number Forty-Four,
and slowly into sunlight sailed
Lady Ottoline, *en grande tenue*, holding herself
as proudly as a rare goose swims;
she was swimming away from the grand and dull,
herself, as ever, too grand to conform.

On her right, the alertest of profiles
fronted the best of brains; her long-boned hand
rested on Bertrand Russell's arm.
On her left, poised on legs
without precedent, Nijinsky himself –
poised as if he could prance for ever
without a thought of any curtain-fall.

Nijinsky, seeing the ballet
of tennis players in white
darting between the tall, theatrical
and sepia-mottled columns of the vaulting trees,
threw out a dancer's arm, and called
in a faun's warm voice
'*Ah, quel décor!*'

The ball slapped into the net. It made the score
a dangerous deuce. A long white ash
dropped from the Baron's cigar. Peace hives
the virus of war. 'Game! And set!'
That moment under the plane trees (*quel décor!*)
was what these lines were cast to recall,
a crystal moment that seemed worth trawling for.

[2]

A VICTORIAN ALBUM

Matriarch, admiral, pert-faced boy,
chlorotic virgin, plethoric bon-vivant,
London dandy, High Church dean or don, two
reposeful sisters (white skins never shown
to the sun, white hands that need never work).

Braid and brocade and broadcloth, made to last;
shrill watered-silk over stiff corsetry;
frock-coats, crinolines, aiglets, galloons, and lace;
costly simplicity; upright backs
against straight-backed chairs; a sword, a Bible, a fan.

Characters! Each (against tasselled drapes,
plaster balusters, pedestals) looked at the lens
with that look on which no sun could ever set,
with a poise derived from pride of birth,
race, class, property, privilege, place.

White, Protestant, English or Scottish,
all these were WE, the rest of the world being THEY –
the low-born or ill-bred, the new rich, the always-
with-us poor; heathens; and foreigners who
from Dover, when clear, could almost be seen to begin.

Turn the page, with your anti-imperial hand.
Who has got among us now? Who on earth
is this? A mahogany-skinned and proud
young Muslim, smiling, handsome, assured.
Thanks to him, I am here to write this today.

That's Osman, who in the Mutiny saved
my grandfather's life, I suppose because
he thought it worth saving. There he stands
great among grandparents, grand among great-
uncles and aunts, he who put friendship first.

NO IDENTITY

Against the name of the place we mean to move to
The guidebook bleakly rules *No identity*:
What Doctor Pevsner means is absence of ancient
Or markworthy buildings.
                              What he implies
Is a shallowly-rooted community, a huddlement
Of not very settled commuters, interspersed with retired
Couples, tending to dwindle to widows,
Little communal sense or parish pride,
And the usual private or commonplace fears
Like that of being moved to some distant branch
Of one's place of work, or of cold old age.

But if a triumphal arch were to welcome us
What better inscription than this, *No identity*?
We are not the sort who wish to reflect prestige
From a rare environment. By possessing antiques
Or using the newest things we feel no need
To reinforce our own identity; at our age
That seems unambiguous enough.
                                  My need
As a poet (not every poet's) is this –
To be immersed in a neutral solution, which
Alone provides an interim, until through the grey
Expectant film invisible writing comes clean.

No identity can be a desirable thing:
To have a face with features noticed less
Than one's range of expression, so that photographed
It never looks twice the same, and people say
'But that's not you!'
                        One would like to reply:
'No, that's not me, because I'm incapable
Of starting the very least personality cult.
I have freed myself at last from being me;
Don't think of me as chameleon or actor; if I take
Protective colouring, it is that I mean to be
A kind of medium, free to enjoy, well, *no identity*.'

ANONYMA

Anxiety dream: late at the
station, train at the
platform, doors all finally
slamming, guard at the
ready, how can I possibly – ?
Exacerbating delay with
ticket, and train about to,
about to, about to
move – but out of it
a hand is waving, I see the smiling
face of Anonyma. All will be well now,
on the train with her;
train leaving.

The train has taken me, taken me
straight out of the dream,
filled with well-being by
reunion with Anonyma.
Waking I remember
she died thirty years ago;
serene, am not awake enough
to feel surprise at
her being alive still.
I see she's immortal.
After thirty years to enter
the dream of a survivor
creatively!

In after years, in some other country,
perhaps I too may smile
welcome in the troubled
sleep of a doubter;
on the cold forehead of solitude
lay four fingers of warmth;
give comfort by my company
to some lone fighter;

271

with this dead hand signal
lively understanding. Just as
she did me, I might hearten someone.
Such a chain-reaction
might have no ending.

THEATRE OF DREAMS

In a cool element of unvarying
shadowless dreamlight,
in a theatre of sinister caprice,
all stage and no audience,
it is here you must act –
to this you have been brought
by lying down under
a sheet of silence, under
a blanket of darkness.

It is a place without reason or logic,
without clock or calendar,
where the dead may be met living
and you may with intense pleasure
enjoy familiarity with strangers,
a place of unforeseeable situations
in which your part is determined
by two dramatists of genius,
collaborators, Fear and Desire.

272

Imagine a play without rehearsals,
the acting impromptu,
long planned, but not put in writing,
a play given one performance
only, in fact only for you.
It's not just entertainment:
the two dramatists, you understand,
are dangerous prisoners, their plays
a substitute for liberation.

TENSION AT SUNSET

A touch of gigantism
is distorting the landscape,
and this on a still day,
cloudless, painted on porcelain.

Huge low-slung spotlight
angled from emptiness, the sun
colours the corals in a hawthorn hedge
and the damson colonies of sloes.

The sunflowers have gone out;
their vertical green pipes
now hold up discs of monochrome mosaic;
these discs look monstrous in the clean air,
itself abnormal in a dirtied world.

The level glare is caught
in the burning glass of a shut
window miles away. One cannot bear
to look at it, nor could one look out of it.

273

Along the bare hillside
the shadow of a tree,
of one small tree,
is a hundred times its length;
its elastic shadow has no breaking-point.
At this moment exaggeration
is seen to be infinite.

This might be the moment,
the right moment for a showdown,
for something postponed
to be made to happen;
but all the long shadows are merging
into one shadow,
into a restless night,
into an unresolved problem
waiting for daylight
to ring its alarm.

[3]

STONES OF ARGYLL

Clans, claymores, cackle about battles,
Jacobites, Covenanters, noisy Knox,
that tall thin nympho Queen of Scots –
all those, to a petrologist, are trash,
newspaper stuff. Newspapers are used
for lighting fires or wrapping fish.

You pick up scraps of gossip out of books:
that's history. Prehistory for me!
Don't misunderstand me if I say 'That's gneiss,'
I'm looking at 300 million years,
at how the world was made. Stones
are what I mean by concrete poetry.

The tide receding from this beach
makes every stone fresher than paint –
cake-like conglomerate, black basalt,
pink granite, purplish andesite,
quartzite, felsite. Gorgeous most
these reddish jaspers with their soapy feel.

FIVE WILD ORCHIDS

'I hunted curious flowers in rapture and muttered thoughts in their praise.'
John Clare]

We won't pick nor let a camera see
these perfect five,
nor tell a single person where they are.

I see their tint and detailed singularity
delineated by a fine, devoted hand
some sunlit sheep-bell afternoon, two centuries ago.

Next year they may increase
or not, along this untouched slope in June,
this unfrequented mild escarpment.

Unlikely we'll be here again
to see the silk-
winged inflorescence on new stems.

We've interrupted their rarity.
With rapture, with praise, with deference
we back away, muttering.

278

IN A CATHEDRAL TOWN

Nothing unusual in the irritable shoving
of one-way traffic through the town
on this technological morning.

Yes, something unusual – a woman
alone on the pavement, in a faded coat,
perhaps forty, with uncombed hair.

She might have been unnoticed,
but raising and lowering a short stick
points repeatedly at a shop opposite.

Ignoring the traffic and passers-by,
aiming her accusing stick, she mutters
incantations, curses.

She has been seen by the shop manager;
with one glossy saleswoman he stares
through plate glass, over the traffic.

Both wear a look of contemptuous amusement,
of superior tolerance, but fail to hide
annoyance and uneasiness at her persistence.

There's no knowing what has provoked her,
nor how long she has been aiming, aiming,
nor whether her manoeuvres are effective.

As if solitude has distilled it,
the witch looks wildly alone with her venom,
erect, independent, a pythoness.

Computers, commuters, cathedral committees
have missed out this other technician
and the assured gestures of primitive magic.

The plate glass may shatter,
the shop fail, the manager collapse,
the saleswoman miscarry.

YOUR HEART AND THE MOON

If, when you gaze at the moon,
about which so many have raved,
your susceptible heart gives a thump,
this proves that a dull desert craved
by yet-to-be far-flung bores
can excite a transplantable pump.
                                    [1968]

TO THE MOON AND BACK

countdown   takeoff
moonprints   rockbox
splashdown   claptrap

280

THE RED FAULT LAMP

The red fault lamp
in the zero reset push-button
is lit on one axis, look,
and it still stays lit
after fault resetting, after checking
it still stays lit:
where do we go from here?

Another thing I don't know
is where should the x and y
oscilloscope input leads be connected
if a check is needed
of the optics signal waveform?
Look at the red fault lamp,
it still stays lit.

Somewhere something is wrong,
as it usually is;
after checking, after resetting
who would ever have thought
the mean little red fault lamp
would still stay lit?
My third question: no answer.

From back there no answer,
nor likely to be now we're this far out
with the moon small as a nut.
Yes, there goes the tiny moon now,
take one last look at it.
And here *we* go, three nuts in space,
with our red fault lamp still lit.

THEY

Do you think about them at all? They
either don't think at all, or think nothing,
or think vaguely of you. They
think what's good to be done or is done well
is only so if done by their own set.

You've been and have done what you could
by being yourself, not one of a set. They
in their zipped-up self-importance
hear your name (they do just hear your name)
condescendingly. Some even praise you.

You once made the mistake you could only
make once, of being young; and so provoked
in them (as they then were) some envy.
Life's motor is habit, so they went on
calling you young till you were bent like a boomerang.

They've stayed unchanged while the usual process
was cutting deep glyphs in your withering face,
but when your hair turned white in a single
decade, they saw it was high time
to disregard you and write you off as stale buns.

As you have for some time built up
what you could against the ravening ebb-tide
with what skill you had and as chance allowed,
and since what you built has form
and is still added to, it's not unknown. They

seeing it not unknown can't quite ignore it. Now,
if they praise, they praise you for what
you're not, or for what they allege you
to have once been. With quaint smugness
they applaud their false image of you.

282

Oddly supposing some judgment needed from them
yet always flummoxed by the imaginative,
or prophetic, or creatively marginal,
they compare it to what they fall for –
the trivial, the trendy, the ephemeral.

If you do happen to waffle on to a great age
they'll allow you a slight curiosity-value
as a survival of a species almost extinct;
they'll patronize you with a show of false esteem,
unaware that you seldom read or hear what they say.

It's plain that by deviating in your own way
you've made what you have. You've made it
clear, durable, pointed as a cluster of crystals. They,
they have grown nothing but a great goitre
of mediocrity – not only unsightly, it's uncurable.

Contemporaries

N., A DIDACTIC JOURNALIST

N. has no time for God; devout
self-worship keeps him quite content.
O God, if able to believe in N.,
You're proved omnipotent.

MRS CANUTE, A REFORMER

Oh for my non-permissive youth!
I shall not rest, as I had planned,
till I have built Tabusalem
In England's mad, unbuttoned land.

POSITIVE

['Positive is the perfection of coxcomb,
he is then come to his full growth.'
                    George Savile, Marquess of Halifax, 1633–95]

His self-esteem has outrun calculation:
you'd make the biggest fortune ever known
if you could buy him at your valuation –
and sell him at his own.

284

[4]

BUREAUCRATIC NEGATIVES

[White South Africans oddly describe themselves as 'Europeans' and black South Africans as 'non-Europeans'. 'If anybody asks me what country I come from,' said a black South African, 'I shall have to say "Non-Europe".' When he asked for a passport he met with a flat refusal. He was told he could have an 'exit permit', entitling him to leave the country but not to return to it.]

What's language for?
I'll tell you what:
it's not to call us what we are
but tell us what we're not.

You can't have a passport,
you're not a non-black:
this permit to go is a
non-permit to come back.

The dead are non-living,
the hungry non-fed:
don't think because you're non-unconscious
that you're alive – you're non-dead.

'[The Publications Control Board has decided to allow South Africans to put ice-cubes made in the shape of female nude dolls into their drinks. Disclosing this information at a women's gathering this week, a member of the Board, Mrs J. P. Theron, said it had been decided to allow the dolly ice-cubes because they melted so quickly in the liquor.

The Board was not narrow-minded, said Mrs Theron.'—*Cape Times*]

What a corrupting new device!
But in this case my ruling is
    Our rules need not be rigid:
These topless girls are bottomless,
And though they give one melting looks
    They're pure. What's more, they're frigid.

WHITE GLOVES

Reading some Russian novel
    far on a Transvaal steppe,
blue hills near in the clean sky's lens
    and Russia brought quite as near
in the focus of prose, the place I was in
    and was not were strangely merged.

Straight as a caryatid
    a brown girl held on her head
a brown girl's burden of white things washed
    for whites, of whom I was one:
she knew she was graceful, I knew
    her life was the life of a serf.

Now, with half a century gone,
    a letter that comes from those parts
shows by its turn and tone of phrase
    it comes from a Tolstoi-time,
from a sun-dried Russia where even now
    the serfs have not yet been freed.

A terrace in lilied shade,
    ice clinks in glasses there,
white gloves disguise black hands that offer
    a tray – untouchable hands.
Cars race to a feast. On the burning veld
    slow peasants stand apart.

The scene dissolves to Kazan:
    the snowy versts race past,
wrapped snug in furs we chatter in French
    as with clinking harness-bells
we drive to a feast. On the frozen road
    slow peasants step aside.

Some other caryatid
   no doubt, after all these years,
barefoot and slow, with patient steps
   in the place I knew upholds
with her strength what has to be done:
   the serfs are not yet freed.

Not of them the letter brings news
   but of a picnic, a bride,
white bride of the son of a millionaire,
   and of pleasures bought. It implies
that a usual social round
   runs on its inbuilt power,

runs by itself, by right;
   will last; must drive, not walk.
Alone and apart, more alone and apart
   it floats, floats high, that world
with the tinted oiliness
   of a bubble's tensile skin:

but inside the bubble a serf,
   black serf, peels off his gloves,
white gloves. With naked hands
   he opens a door FOR WHITES ALONE
and salutes in a mirror the self
   he is destined at last to meet.

[5]

THE GURU

The father figures lie in broken pieces,
broken eggshells
out of which we had to break away.
The pedestals they stood on
serve as paving stones.

Old men! We talk to them
but they're not listening,
they're looking inwards,
listening to the past.

Old men! Each a city in himself,
he listens to the traffic that he knows,
his arteries are memories,
every corpuscle a human face.

Old men! They know you're free,
they're longing to control you,
they judge you,
they condemn you,
they're longing to reform you.

And yet among them is the guru.
You can recognize the guru:
he respects you,
he accepts you.

Purged of conceit
and far beyond resentment,
he won't condemn us.
How can he,
when he knows in each of us
has been, is, or may be
the seed of every other?

When we don't know what we're doing
but think we know,
the guru lays his patience as a path
for us to walk on
if we want to.

He learns by teaching,
and calmly he can view
among his million other selves
the self that's you.

ANOTHER OLD MAN

'On my ancestor's tomb
this epitaph's cut:
HE WAS UPRIGHT, MODEST, AND AFFABLE.
That's possible, but
let my epitaph say:

SOMETIMES THINKING ALOUD
HE WENT HIS OWN WAY.
HE WAS JOKY BY NATURE,
SAD, SCEPTICAL, PROUD.
WHAT HE NEVER WOULD FOLLOW,
OR LEAD, WAS A CROWD.'

AT A MEMORIAL SERVICE

All here are formalists.
In the cruciform church
all stand facing east. All kneel.
Each muffles his faith, or no faith,
in old clean robes of prayer.
All attend, as words model
an image of a man they remember.
Here and there in a grey head
remembrance now stings
disused lachrymal ducts.

As a death brings them back to
their inherited cult
those decent grey heads,
respectful, respected,
conforming, are calmed.
One man less, they're estranged
that much more from the angry
menace outside,
the mad new Establishment
of loud disrespect.

As they rise to intone
an articulate hymn,
beneath it, in unison,
breathes a vast sighing
out of old tribal times:
migrant birds over oceans
rush, not knowing why,
their consensus of confidence
one soft brush touching
danger, day, and the dark.

PUT UP TO BE SHOT AT

Your life is a target
exposed to a marksman
who shoots when he feels like it.

There's no doubt who he is,
and it's no good supposing
anything can stop him.

When you think him asleep, he may
take aim again, casually
nicking an outer.

After years of immunity
you may end up as full of
holes as a colander.

Or even now one shot may
punch through the heart of you
a peephole at infinity.

But would you wish to be
never at all shot at?
Isn't that unthinkable?

296

SLEEPING ALONE

Needing night's amnesia
she folds the sheet about her shoulder
and the dark across her eyes,
but the sinking pillow is a trap,
leaves her utterly alone,
unprotected, to her dreams.

Though a folded wing of hair
guards her eyelids, though a guarding
arm is round her, there she dreams
dreaded dreams which resurrect the dead:
courage cannot ever make her
stronger than those revenants.

DEATH OF A HEDGE-SPARROW

This afternoon it stood alone
Beside me, showed no fear,
Resting its head between its wings.
After an hour it moved, it fell,
Under a tower of leaves
Careened, and there it lay.

There as it lay, its thin,
Its thorn-fine claws
Encircled emptiness;
Its dew-bright eyes began
To blur. Its pin-point beak
Drank three quick sips of air.

Then it half seemed to sigh,
Stretched with (too faint to hear)
One last, fan-opening whirr
To full extent both wings,
In flight from life;
They slowly closed.
It shivered once; lay still.

To mind there sprang
A Roman phrase, *Ubi humilitas*,
Ibi majestas. Great marble word
For an almost weightless corpse!
My little pang was not excess
Of sentiment, it was proportionate
(Sole witness, I affirm) to what I saw.

NOW

1

Lonely old woman, her husband died
on some useless alp.
Lonely old woman, widow
of a lost civilization.

A prisoner of habit, at home
she has lived on and on, inside a dream
of her safe early years
in a lost civilization.

This once quiet by-road's now a by-pass.
Her well-built house stands well back
half hidden by trees,
and not yet for sale.

'Rare opportunity,'
some agent will announce,
'gracious detached
character residence of older type,
might suit institution, requires
some modernization,'
having been planned for
a lost civilization.

Prodding and peeping in this acre of jungle,
once a garden, a modernizer
may break his leg, snared
by a rusty croquet-hoop
or the lead rim of a half buried
ornamental cistern.
There's no gardener now.

Like the house its owners
were gracious, detached,
thought it wiser not to love

299

one's neighbour as oneself,
wisest
to be only upon nodding terms.

As clear as an inscription
their thoughts could be read:

> *Presuming on propinquity*
> *neighbours might show themselves,*
> *might show curiosity,*
> *or, by asking questions,*
> *familiarity.*

> *How appalling*
> *if they were to speak*
> *about themselves!*
> *They might try and impress one,*
> *or, absurdly, pretend*
> *one couldn't impress them –*
> *as if one would ever bother*
> *to make the attempt!*

> *I suppose if appealed to*
> *in some crisis*
> *one might be driven,*
> *yes, driven by imprudence,*
> *to play the Samaritan.*

2

Under the heavier and heavier alluvium of noise
deafness has silted up and sealed the house.
In unremembered, as if Etruscan, painted rooms
rare and hand-made undiscovered things are waiting,
finely made to last, things handed down
and kept with the respectful care of those
accustomed to good things – things touched and seen
almost as if animate, things heartfelt.

300

To have assets or have food to eat
was once inseparable from thanks; wastefulness
by rich or poor, so it was taught,
was wrong; but avarice was despised.
Now by-pass lives are caught up in a complex
of invented needs that money-suckers boost
for quantities of trash, fallible,
expendable, much of it indestructible.

First thing in the morning, drawing back
threadbare curtains to light her loveless days,
habit makes her note the night's additions
to the day's, to every day's, disjections:
over her straggled hedge bottles and cartons fly,
cans, another broken mattress, one more white
up-ended broken stove, and nameless things,
conglomerating a malignant growth.

3

'Horner has died, who used to put things right
and keep things straight for me, and keep things clean,
and make things grow. He fought for tidiness
against the weather, gales, weeds, pests.
"Mustn't let Nature have her way," he said.
He knew that gardening is an art. I used to think
he seemed in the garden like a worshipper,
bowed down and kneeling all those devoted years.

'Now Mrs Horner's gone. Twice the corner wall
of Mrs Horner's cottage quite collapsed
under the impact of a ten-wheeled lorry.
Neither time was Mrs Horner, who did everything
for me, there in the room. So fortunate!
"It would be tempting Providence," she said,
"to use that room again." After repairs
she always kept it locked, and empty too.

'In this house now I only use two rooms.
Thanks to my deafness, I don't hear them now,
those dreadful lorries, like warehouses going by,
and motor-bicycles, so fast, the wild young men
fly past with streaming hanks of hair
jerking back in the wind like snakes,
and frantic fringes on their leather coats –
off to their coven, I fancy, on some blasted heath.'

4

'As for me, I never mope.
I dodge self-pity like the plague.
Hope? A drug I'm now immune to.
I expect to finish here, alone.
If I collapse, am found, and driven away,
what good would that do? None.

'I'm light as a feather now,
dry papery skin, and like my mother
I'm small-boned.
I can imagine after a long delay
forcible entry, and what was me on the floor
like a discarded summer travelling-coat,

'or like a dried-up butterfly
(butterflies never learn that the finest fidgeting
continued and continued even all summer long
can never make that wall of solid air,
a sheet of glass, a sudden
change to freedom),

'or like the sloughed skin of a snake
(I hope I may say non-poisonous).
Lying there, I'll be proved less durable
than my Tudor spoon, my Hilliard,
or my melon-slice of jade.
Exquisite, isn't it?

'One hope I have, that these few pretty things
inherited or acquired, outlasting me,
may be cherished for what they are
more than for what they'd fetch.
Who, you may ask, is to inherit them?
Leaving the world, I leave them to the world.'

ml